Teaching
Word Analysis
Skills

Authors
Ashley Bishop, Ed.D., and Sue Bishop, M.E.D.
Foreword by Lance M. Gentile, Ph.D.

Teaching Word Analysis Skills

Editor
Kristy Stark, M.A.Ed.

Assistant Editor
Leslie Huber, M.A.

Editorial Director
Lori Kamola, M.S.Ed.

Editor-in-Chief
Sharon Coan, M.S.Ed.

Editorial Manager
Gisela Lee, M.A.

**Creative Director/
Cover Design**
Lee Aucoin

Print Production Manager
Don Tran

Interior Layout Designer
Robin Erickson

Publisher
Corinne Burton, M.A.Ed.

Shell Education

5301 Oceanus Drive
Huntington Beach, CA 92649-1030

http://www.shelleducation.com

ISBN 978-1-4258-0473-2

© 2010 Shell Education

Reprinted 2011

Table of Contents

Foreword

Ashley Bishop and Sue Bishop have written a unique and timely book in literacy. Unlike many others in the field whose sole focus is "cracking the code," *Teaching Word Analysis Skills* takes the reader to a broader and deeper understanding of the topic.

The authors note that each student learns to problem solve new and unfamiliar words when reading and writing in his or her own way. They say that to be effective, students must learn to identify unknown words using more than phonics. While phonics is an important and useful tool in word analysis, it is not always efficient. Unlike Spanish and other more harmonious sound-to-letter languages, English has many irregular correspondences. This does not mean that phonics should not be taught because systematic and explicit phonic instruction is an integral part of learning to read and write. But, word analysis can at times be a rule-defying, greater-than-the-sum-of-the-parts, alchemy-involving *language, literacy* and *learning behavior*.

Language: This book also cites the importance of phonemic awareness in analyzing words. Learning to identify and use the sounds of language to communicate thoughts, feelings, and intentions meaningfully and to tie them to what is read or written is essential. Bishop and Bishop identify problems at the sound level as some of the most obvious indicators of early difficulties in literacy.

The authors emphasize that students lacking phonological strengths struggle with word analysis and consequently may not engage in conceptually challenging literacy tasks that require them to read, write, and wrestle with unfamiliar words found in books. Identifying and using the phonemes of language to decode and encode print accurately and fluently to comprehend and express ideas clearly, both verbally and in writing, is of signal importance to success in school.

But, too much emphasis on phonic or phonemic development and the repetitive testing for these skills can force teachers to overlook the importance of integrating instruction with real literature.

In Chapter 10, the authors note that this is especially true when it comes to working with English language learners. They introduce 10 key issues related to teaching word analysis skills to these students and present instructional strategies for effective intervention. While, unquestionably, word analysis skills are important for all students, this is not the most critical need in English language learners' acquisition of literacy. They are best served by more time spent on language development rather than analyzing phonic or phonemic elements. *Teaching Word Analysis Skills* contains multiple examples of how to combine decoding skills instruction with whole text and authentic reading and writing activities.

Literacy and Learning Behavior: This book points out that unlike the "real" world in which students live, where an apple or chair turned sideways or upside down remains an apple or chair, there is no such flexibility in looking at or producing print. Perhaps the most underestimated feature of learning to read and write concerns psychomotor development. This means that word analysis is conducted according to an arbitrary system of left-to-right sequencing or serial order, and students must automatically conform to patterned, directional constraints. Learning where to start looking at new or unfamiliar words and which way to go is requisite to the fluent parsing and comprehension of written words.

Bishop and Bishop highlight the fact that word analysis is a language, thinking, personal-and-problem solving, constructive process. When students do not possess flexible strategies to approach analyzing words, literacy becomes a laborious, time-consuming, and meaningless task. Ultimately, they may perceive reading and writing as overly difficult or threatening and develop negative responses that prompt them to confront or retreat from learning.

The authors emphasize comprehension and fluency as being the basis for teaching students to analyze words. They tie learning directly to interest. Students are more apt to learn to identify unfamiliar or difficult words and work at figuring them out when they are reading or writing what interests them. No one spends a good deal of time and focused energy looking at or studying something uninteresting.

In my 42 years of teaching English speakers, as well as English language learners at every level, I have not read a more clear and thorough discussion of the importance of teaching how to identify new and unfamiliar words than what is offered in *Teaching Word Analysis Skills*. Teachers and students of every age and description will benefit greatly from the approach Bishop and Bishop present to the philosophy and practical application of instruction in this compact and comprehensive text.

Lance M. Gentile Ph.D., Professor Emeritus,
Language and Literacy,
San Francisco State University

Preface

My wife and coauthor asked me to write a few more words about the concepts contained in *Teaching Word Analysis Skills.* She did so for a very special reason— what is contained in this book has great significance to me. My elementary school years were not the most pleasant. I completed the first grade once, was asked to participate in the second grade twice, and based on my academic performance, it would not have been inappropriate to have been in the third grade three times. By the time I arrived at the sixth grade, I was a charter member of the low group and developed the attitude that reading was an activity to avoid at all cost. In fact, I viewed reading only as a series of skills that resulted in failure. Obviously, reading was my least favorite subject. Fortunately, as I moved into my final year of elementary school, Mr. Winters made the decision that I could and would read.

One day, while I was leaping benches during the lunch hour (unfortunately, students were still sitting at the benches), Mr. Winters noticed my interest in hurdling. That very day, he presented me with a book about a track star with perfect hurdling form who wanted to win the city championships. That afternoon, at the end of the school day, he read the first chapter to me and then sent both me and the book home. Let me say, I wanted to read that book! I struggled through it three times until I could understand every wonderful concept and every bit of action presented. I was hooked, and Mr. Winters had more bait. He presented me with one sports book after another and then introduced me to the library. He told me that I could read any book in this place of amazing knowledge if I would just take the time to really learn the skills of reading. I could read anything and find out anything, and I could do it myself!

My remembrances lead me to the point of *Teaching Word Analysis Skills.* Students often see little reason to learn about schwas, digraphs, and diphthongs. They want to read books about large red dogs, curious monkeys, and teachers who come from black lagoons. Great literature motivates students to learn important and necessary decoding skills. If students are going to develop the richest possible "logic of the code," we must give them both reasons and skills to do so, just as Mr. Winters did for me.

This book is an expansion and update of a text, *Teaching Phonics, Phonemic Awareness, and Word Recognition*, that we wrote several years ago. The new title, *Teaching Word Analysis Skills*, was selected because we felt that *word analysis* better reflects the role students have as they engage in the decoding process. Students must have the skills, confidence, and personal commitment to not just pronounce words but also to carefully analyze words as they look to understand and enjoy the material they are reading. The organization of *Teaching Word Analysis Skills* is as follows:

Chapter One looks at the role of word analysis. The phrase *analysis process* is defined, and our philosophy that it must be seen as a personal process is presented. **Chapter Two** discusses the reading/writing process. It contains specific information concerning decoding and comprehension. **Chapter Three** deals with phonemic awareness and **Chapter Four** with the alphabet. Phonics is discussed in **Chapter Five**, including a history, definition, and specific suggested strategies. **Chapters Six, Seven, and Eight** focus on structural analysis, sight words, and context clues, respectively. **Chapter Nine** examines fluency and its importance to both word analysis and comprehension. **Chapter Ten** provides a summary of key text concepts and discusses instructional strategies and accommodations appropriate for English Language Learners. We conclude with references and a listing of children's books cited. At the end of each chapter, important points are highlighted and questions for reflection are included. We wish you good reading and teaching.

—Ashley Bishop and Sue Bishop

Chapter 1

Word Analysis

A Personal Perspective

We wrote this book for a very pragmatic reason. We want students, when encountering unfamiliar words, to have all the word analysis skills necessary to pronounce and understand them. We do not care if these skills are learned implicitly or explicitly or in a student-centered or skill-based classroom. Students need to develop their own logic of how the code process works and have the desire and confidence to use the process whenever it is needed. We do have a bias about the environment in which to best teach students the necessary word analysis skills. It is a balanced environment where students are given authentic reasons to read and write and are systematically provided with instruction that allows them to do so. In a *Reading Teacher* article titled "My Daughter Learns to Read" (Bishop 1978), we asked educators to "neither simpleminded nor muddleheaded be." Our concern was this: "As we put added emphasis on the basics, there are teachers forgetting to give students a reason for reading. This is being simpleminded. Supplying students with a set of skills does not necessarily produce readers. On the flip side of the coin, there are teachers who feel that all one must do is put a book in students' hands, love them, read to them often, and they will learn to read. These teachers have forgotten the necessity of using skills in reading. This is being muddleheaded" (Bishop 1978, 6).

Simpleminded and muddleheaded are strong terms to use, but they reflect the degree of our disenchantment in 1978 over the bitterness of the reading debate. The essence of the debate focused on the role of phonics in the word analysis process. The focus of the debate now has shifted. There is agreement that phonics should have a central role in reading instruction, but there is disagreement on how best and how long to teach phonics. In this text, we will focus extensively on phonics and provide answers on how best and how long to teach this important component of the word analysis process.

The text title, *Teaching Word Analysis Skills,* accurately reflects its content. We want to present a clear definition of word analysis and productive strategies for teaching necessary skills. The meaning of *word analysis* has varied definitions in the field of education. In this text, it will be defined as follows:

> *the process of identifying a word not immediately recognized by the reader*

As presented earlier, phonics will receive careful and extensive attention, but structural analysis and context, equally important components of the word analysis process, will also be addressed in depth. When examining the word analysis process, we also feel it is essential to look carefully at the importance of alphabet knowledge, phonemic awareness, sight words, and fluency. Alphabet knowledge and phonemic awareness are central to the successful learning of phonics. Some words cannot be analyzed successfully and must be learned by sight, and fluency is a critical bridge to comprehension. Ultimately, to be successful readers, students must develop their own understanding of how our language works and then be able to decode words so fluently and naturally that all attention is given to understanding what is being read. This happens best when students have been systematically taught all the skills necessary to successfully analyze words. This book presents these skills.

Important Points to Remember

- Word analysis can be defined as the process of identifying a word not immediately recognized by the reader.

- Students need to develop their own logic of how the word analysis process works and have the desire and confidence to use the process whenever needed.

- Supplying students with a set of skills does not necessarily produce readers.

Post-Reading Reflection

1. What word analysis skills are most essential for your students?

2. State your opinion on a balanced approach to teaching reading.

Chapter 2

The Reading and Writing Process

Printed Language

To appropriately discuss the role that analyzing words plays in the reading process, it is important to have a clear understanding of what authors do as they engage in the writing process and what readers do as they engage in the reading process. Authors have thoughts, ideas, feelings, and concerns. They turn all of these concepts into language and put this language on the printed page. Readers must lift this printed language off the page and interact with the ideas being presented, as well as construct new and personalized meaning. We say, then, that reading is a process of active communication in which students construct knowledge from an author's printed language.

Reading is an act of constructing knowledge from what is read. A variety of processes in which readers must engage to be successful are necessary. The following page presents these processes.

The Processes of Reading

Reading as a Language Process

Readers are communicating with an author's printed language. To be able to read, one must have language. The more this language is like that of the author's printed language, the greater the chance that active communication will take place.

Reading as a Thinking Process

Without thinking, active communication cannot take place. Active communication is the process that readers use to seek meaning. When the meaning being sought is personally valuable, the reading process is more active. In short, readers have questions that they want answered. In fact, one of the significant differences between good readers and poor readers is that good readers have a personal stake in their reading. They are involved in the process because they want to be. They read because they want to be entertained or they have questions that they want answered. If there is one statement that summarizes good readers, it is this—good readers ask questions. The questions they should ask are questions that move their thinking well beyond the literal level. The best questions that they can ask are often "What is the author's purpose in writing this?" and "How effectively did the author achieve this purpose?" This is sophisticated thinking, but young readers do it all the time. When they say, "I like Clifford books. They are funny," students are understanding that the author's purpose is to entertain. When they say, "I want to read more books by Norman Bridwell," they are stating that they think he is an effective writer.

Reading as a Decoding Process

Readers must have a variety of tools to lift the author's printed language off the page. Decoding supplies students with such tools. When students use context clues, phonics, and structural analysis, have a rich store of sight words, and read fluently, they have the resources to change printed language into thoughts and ideas with which they can communicate. Ultimately, the decoding process should be so natural and fluent that all attention is focused on understanding what is read.

Reading as a Personal Process

Reading is one of the most personal processes in which individuals can engage. The meaning readers take away from the printed page is often unique. The more the reader's knowledge of the world is like that of the author, the more easily communication will take place. Also, reading is a personal process in relation to the physical and mental health of readers. When students are feeling good both mentally and physically, reading is a less difficult task. When they are tired, hungry, and unsure of themselves, communicating with printed language can seem to be an overwhelming task. We have all found that studying for three final exams in a row can be a significant challenge in the best of cases, and it is almost impossible when we lack sleep, proper nutrition, and confidence. Finally, students' attitudes toward reading and their views of themselves as readers make reading very much a personal process. We know that students view themselves as readers when they walk into the classroom and say, "Wow, a new book by Jack Prelutsky! Can I read it?"

Reading as a Constructive Process

One of the most important results of the reading process is that readers leave the printed page with more knowledge than they started with. For this to happen, students must bring experiences, concepts, language, and motivation to the reading task and must use each of these to test what they are reading against what they already know and what they would like to learn. As students say, "This makes sense," "I didn't know this," or "This is just what I needed to know," they are constructing knowledge. This is the heart of the reading process.

The Components of Reading

For discussion purposes, reading can be broken into two major components: word analysis and comprehension. Word analysis and comprehension seem to be mutually enriching tasks, and, while it is often difficult to separate the two, they will be discussed separately.

Word Analysis

The word analysis process can be separated into broad categories: phonics, structural analysis, sight words, and context clues.

Phonics is the association of sounds with symbols. The printed word *cat* is made up of three symbols: the letters of the alphabet *c*, *a*, and *t*. Students use phonics to attach the sounds /k/, /a/, and /t/ to these symbols. Because our alphabet consists of consonants and vowels, phonics is the process of giving sounds to single consonants, consonant clusters, single vowels, and vowel clusters.

Structural analysis is the analysis of the structure of a word. While phonics is reasonably successful with single-syllable words, it begins to break down with multisyllabic words. Consequently, the task of structural analysis is to break large words into more manageable units. For example, when seeing the word *cowboy* for the first time, students will often notice the smaller units *cow* and *boy*. The term *morphemic analysis* is often used in place of structural analysis.

The definition of sight words rivals the logic of the definition of structural analysis. Sight words are words that are recognized immediately without the need of analysis. Sight words are important for a variety of reasons, but most significantly because a majority of the words students frequently encounter cannot be sounded out. Words such as *was*, *said*, *the*, and *to* do not effectively subject themselves to the use of phonics. Ultimately, the goal is for all words to become sight words.

Using context clues means using the print surrounding an unfamiliar word to give it meaning and to help pronounce it. When students are reading the sentence "The _____ is a lizard that changes color," they quite often will insert *chameleon* because they know that word makes sense.

Educators want to produce readers who use word analysis skills so naturally and fluently that all of their attention is on gathering meaning from what is being read. For this to happen, students must understand the process so well that they develop their own logic of the code. No two students approach an unknown word in exactly the same way. They take the tools they have been taught and personalize the process by using the ones that make the most sense and that work best for them. It is our task to ensure that students have been taught all of the essential word analysis options so that the personal logic of the code process that they develop is as rich as possible.

Comprehension

Comprehension is the heart of the reading process. When involved in the comprehension process, students test what they read against what they already know. Stated another way, comprehension results from the interaction between the information in the text and the prior knowledge readers bring to the text. This is the act of comprehension or the process of constructing knowledge. As students comprehend, they need to do so at three levels, each more important than the one preceding it.

Reading the Lines

Reading the lines is the process of comprehending at the "who," "what," "where," and "when" level. It is understanding information that is explicitly stated. The often-asked questions, "Who is buried in Grant's tomb?" or "What color is Clifford, the dog?" are reading-the-lines level questions. These types of questions are lower-level questions and are often labeled literal reading. Students can function at this level quite successfully and still not really understand what they are reading.

Reading Between the Lines

Reading between the lines is often labeled interpretive reading, and it is at this level that critical or higher-order thinking takes place. Students who function at this level make inferences about implicit text information. Answering the question, "Which of the three little pigs is the smartest?"—when the answer is not explicitly stated in the story—is an example of reading between the lines.

Reading Beyond the Lines

Reading beyond the lines asks students to step outside the story and view it from another perspective. There are several components to reading beyond the lines: application, creative, critical, and evaluative reading.

- Application reading is the process that uses what is gained from the text material in a real-life situation or compares what is learned to other text material.

- Creative reading is the process of manipulating the story in creative ways. Coming up with another ending to a story, seeing the story from a different perspective, or changing the personality of the main character and seeing how this might change the direction of the story are all creative endeavors.

- Critical reading, in its richest form, is understanding the author's purpose. "Why is the author writing this?" is an important critical-level question for readers to ask.

- Evaluative reading is making a judgment on how effectively the author did what he or she wanted to do.

Combining these last two levels of comprehension, *reading between the lines* and *reading beyond the lines*, it can be said that a critical-evaluative reader is one who understands what the author is doing and how effectively the author does it. This is truly higher-order thinking.

Concluding Remarks

In review, the components of reading are comprehension and word analysis. They are often difficult to separate and are mutually enriching tasks. An important concept to remember is that *comprehension is what reading is about*. Students must read for meaning. That is, they must acknowledge and anticipate that they are reading to gain information.

Word analysis is a tool that is learned and used to help readers comprehend. It is a necessary skill that assists readers in identifying unknown words. It must be accompanied by a quest for comprehension if reading is to be a meaningful experience. Too often, students become engrossed with the task of analyzing words and lose sight of the purpose—to understand what they are reading. As teachers, we must ensure that students develop an appreciation for reading and recognize that while analyzing words is important, it is only one part of the process. Both comprehension and the word analysis process are vital for success.

Important Points to Remember

- Readers must lift an author's printed language off the page and interact with the ideas being presented, as well as construct new and personalized meaning.

- Active communication is the process that readers use to seek meaning.

- One of the most important results of the reading process is that readers leave the printed page with more knowledge than they brought to it.

- Comprehension results from the interaction between the information in the text and the prior knowledge readers bring to the text.

- An important concept to remember is that comprehension is the main purpose for reading.

Post-Reading Reflection

1. Which of the processes of reading do you think that you teach well?

2. Which processes are areas of needed improvement in your classroom?

3. Does your current definition of reading include a balance of word analysis and comprehension skills?

4. Does your teaching reflect this balance?

....

Chapter 3

Phonemic Awareness

....

One of the essential components of the word analysis process is phonics. We must remember that one goal of phonics instruction is to assist students in understanding the relationship between printed letters and speech sounds. Therefore, this chapter discusses the concept of phonemic awareness—awareness of the sounds in our language. The chapter that follows focuses on printed letters—our alphabet. These chapters must precede a discussion on phonics in order to develop a rich understanding of the process students go through as they associate sounds (phonemes) with symbols (graphemes).

To begin a chapter on phonemic awareness, we need to define it and stress its importance. We particularly like Yopp and Stapleton's definition: "Phonemic awareness is the insight that the speech streams consist of individual sounds, or phonemes. It is the ability to attend to and manipulate these smallest sounds of spoken language." (Yopp and Stapleton 2008, 374). Adams (1990) tells us that it is not a working knowledge of phonemes but conscious, analytic knowledge that is so important. It is neither the ability to hear the differences between two phonemes nor the ability to distinctly produce them that is significant. What is important is the awareness that they exist as abstract and manipulative components of our language. Developmentally, this awareness seems to depend upon a student's inclination or encouragement to lend conscious attention to the sounds, as distinct from the meaning of words.

The importance of phonemic awareness to reading success cannot be stressed enough. Research has shown repeatedly that phonics is a potent predictor of success in learning to read (Adams 1990; Stanovich 1986; Yopp 1988; Yopp 1995b). Stanovich (1986) tells us that phonemic awareness is more highly related to reading success than students' scores on intelligence and reading readiness tests and on their listening/comprehension performance. What is exciting about phonemic awareness, given its importance, is that it can be developed in students through training. The International Reading Association (1998) states its position about phonemic awareness and explains that research appears to support the concept that the acquisition of phonemic awareness occurs over time and develops gradually into more and more sophisticated levels and that approximately 80 percent of children develop phonemic awareness by the middle of the first grade. Yopp (1992) suggests the following progression in phonemic awareness training:

Guide students to...
1. hear rhymes or alliteration.
2. blend sounds to produce a spoken word.
3. count phonemes in spoken words.
4. identify the beginning, middle, and final sounds in spoken words.
5. substitute one phoneme for another.
6. delete phonemes from words.
7. segment words into phonemes.

This is labeled a progression because each task is somewhat more challenging than the task preceding it. Teachers should guide students through this progression in preschool, kindergarten, and early first grade. However, a small number of students may need phonemic training well into their later school years. A word of caution: While we are suggesting that some students need training in phonemic knowledge, we are not suggesting word/sound drills and worksheets. What we are suggesting is language play—fully immersing children in rhymes, rhythms, word play, and rich, predictable literature. The following section will present activities that develop phonemic awareness in children.

Strategies for Developing Phonemic Awareness

The following strategies relate to the seven-step progression presented on page 26. In each activity, the focus is on promoting active involvement by the students.

1. Hear rhymes or alliteration

On the first rainy day of the year, read students *Rain Talk* by Serfozo (1993). As the rain falls outside the window, talk about the sounds that rain makes as it hits different surfaces. Then read students poems that deal with the rain. We suggest Prelutsky's *The Random House Book of Poetry for Children* (1983). Students especially enjoy the poems "The Muddy Puddle" and "Mud." The poem "Mud" begins, "Mud is very nice to feel all squishy-squash between the toes! I'd rather wade in wiggly mud than smell a yellow rose" (Prelutsky 1983, 28). Talk about how the words *toes* and *rose* rhyme. Discuss with students other words that rhyme with *toes* and *rose* and then play a game called "I Say, You Say." Say a word and then ask for volunteers to say a word that rhymes with it. Begin by saying *book*, and then ask for a volunteer. He or she might volunteer *cook*. Praise the response, and then have the whole class respond with *cook* when you say *book*. Continue with another four or five words, and have the whole class respond after a volunteer responds. A fun option is to have the volunteer be the teacher and say his or her word and the whole class responds with the original word that the teacher presented to the class.

2. Blend sounds to produce a spoken word

Play the "Slow Way, Fast Way" game. Tell the class that you will say a word the slow way and they can say it back to you the fast way. When you first do this, put the word in a familiar context. Tell students that you are visiting a farm and on the farm you see a /d/-/u/-/k/, extending the word by its sounds. Ask students to think for a moment about what you might have seen. Then say the sounds again and have the class respond as a group. Do the same with *cow*, *pig*, and any other farm animals that are appropriate.

3. Count phonemes in spoken words

Have students each place a blank sheet of paper and a pencil on their desks. Tell them that you are going to walk across the classroom while saying your name very slowly. Have them make a mark every time they hear you say a sound in your name. Stand with your back against one wall, and then walk slowly toward the other wall while you say your name. As you say your name sound by extended sound, hold up a finger for each sound you make. Tell students to listen for sounds and to watch your fingers. Remind students that they should make a mark for each sound they hear. Next, have a student volunteer do the same thing with his or her name, but have students in the classroom raise their fingers as the volunteer slowly walks across the classroom. Praise individual students as appropriate. Once students are comfortable with the process, have students use new sheets of paper, write their names on them, and number from one to three on the papers. Slowly pronounce three words and tell students to make marks for each sound they hear. Finally, next to their names at the top of the papers, have students write the number of sounds in their own names. Collect their papers and check for success. When you feel students are successful, ask them to select words from the word wall or from words they have heard in favorite stories, pronounce the words, and tell you the number of sounds they hear.

4. **Identify beginning, middle, and final sounds in spoken words**

In this activity, students listen to a song that encourages them to think about sounds in words. The teacher may choose to emphasize a single sound throughout the song, or each verse may focus on a different sound. Songs can also focus on medial or final sounds. The following verse, sung to the tune of "Old MacDonald Had a Farm," is an excellent example of the process.

What's the sound that starts these words:
Turtle, time, and *teeth*?
/t/ is the sound that starts these words:
Turtle, time, and *teeth*.
With a /t/, /t/ here, and a /t/, /t/ there,
Here a /t/, there a /t/, everywhere a /t/, /t/.
/t/ is the sound that starts these words:
Turtle, time, and *teeth*!
(Yopp 1992, 700)

5. **Substitute one phoneme for another**

Take class attendance or have students line up when you call their names. However, when you call their names, replace the initial sounds with a sound that begins the name of one of the other students in your class. For example, say, "Today we're going to think about the sound that begins Pablo's name." Ask for volunteers to name this sound. Once students are comfortable with the /p/ sound in isolation, tell them that you will call on them by using the /p/ sound instead of the sound that really begins their names. Model by saying, "Today I will be Mr. Pishop instead of Mr. Bishop." Then call on "Parla" and "Parlos." Extend the initial sound as you say their names. Hopefully, these students will recognize that you are calling them and both come forward. Explain to the class that you replaced the sounds at the beginning of their names with the /p/ sound. Once students are comfortable with the process, call roll or have students line up for recess with this process. In addition, read Silverstein's (2005) *Runny Babbit* to students.

6. **Delete phonemes from words**

Continue the above process except eliminate a sound from student names. Model the process by telling the students that today you will be Mr. Ishop. Ask for a volunteer to tell what sound is missing from your name. Praise as appropriate, then extend the /b/ sound as you place it at the beginning of *ishop,* producing *Bishop*. Once students are comfortable with the process, ask *arla* and *arlos* to come to the board. Ask both to say their names with their missing beginning sounds pronounced in an extended manner. As students get comfortable with the process, delete ending and middle sounds from words.

7. **Segment words into phonemes**

Tell students that you will call on them by saying their name in a special way. It would be best to initially call on students whose names have only two or three sounds. When you say their names, prolong each sound. As students become more comfortable with the process, call on students with longer names. Since you want students to be able to produce the sounds in words, the next step is important. Return to the song "Old MacDonald Had a Farm." Sing the song as it was originally intended, but instead of saying, "And on that farm he had a *cow*," simply say the sounds in the word *cow* and have students guess the animal. When appropriate, call on volunteers to provide an animal, but instead of saying the animal's name, have student provide the sounds. You and the class sing, "And on that farm he had a ..." and the volunteer responds, /p/-/i/-/g/. You and the class sing, "*pig*." Take plenty of time to guide students through this process. Before starting phonics instruction, be sure that students have fully conquered the segmenting process. Finally, give students the opportunity to write using invented spelling. This is a wonderful way to enhance their ability to segment words.

Assessing Phonemic Awareness

Yopp developed the Yopp-Singer test of phonemic awareness. Yopp indicates that students who segment all or nearly all of the words correctly are probably phonemically aware. While the test is presented in Appendix A, we strongly suggest that teachers who want to use the test read the complete article titled "A Test For Assessing Phonemic Awareness in Young Children" (Yopp 1995b).

The Yopp-Singer test is presented as a game for students to play. To administer the test, students are told that they are going to play a word game and they will have a chance to break apart words. Students are given the example *old*, and the person administering the test tells them how to break apart the word using sounds (e.g., /o/-/l/-/d/). Then the test administrator reads each of the words to the student. The student does not see the list of words, but he or she is given each word orally. Words that the student can break apart correctly are circled on the test, while words that are segmented incorrectly are left blank.

Literature That Promotes Phonemic Awareness

Throughout this book, we will provide lists of children's books that enhance the skill being discussed. For a comprehensive selection of books that promote phonemic awareness, read the article *Read-Aloud Books for Developing Phonemic Awareness: An Annotated Bibliography* (Yopp 1995a). The following includes a list of some of our favorite books for promoting phonemic awareness:

I Love You, Good Night by Jon Buller and Susan Schade
A mother and child tell each other how much they love each other with phrases such as, "as much as pigs love pies" and "as much as frogs love flies."

Who Is Tapping at My Window? by A. G. Deming
A young girl hears a tapping at her window and asks, "Who is there?" The animals respond. The loon is followed by the raccoon; the dog is followed by the frog.

Llama, Llama Mad at Mama by Anna Dewdney
This is a sequel to *Llama, Llama Red Pajama* where Llama Llama gets mad at Mama when forced to go clothes shopping. It is full of appealing rhymes.

Stop That Noise! by Paul Geraghty
A mouse is annoyed with a noisy forest. The presentation of animal and machine noises draw attention to the sounds of our language.

Six Sleepy Sheep by Jeffie Ross Gordon
Six sheep try to fall asleep by slurping celery soup and sipping simmered milk. This book helps students practice and become aware of the /s/ sound.

I Can Fly by Ruth Krauss
In this simple book, a child imitates the actions of a variety of animals. "A cow can moo. I can too." On the final page, nonsense words that rhyme are used, encouraging listeners

to experiment with sounds. "Gubble gubble gubble, I'm a mubble in a pubble."

Buzz Said the Bee by Wendy Lewison
A series of animals sits on top of each other. Before each animal climbs on top, it does something that rhymes with the animal it approaches. The hen dances a jig on the pig.

Dinosaur Chase by Carolyn Otto
A mother dinosaur reads her child a story about dinosaurs. Both alliteration and rhyme are used.

A Giraffe and a Half by Shel Silverstein
Using cumulative and rhyming patterns, this story is about a giraffe who has a rose on his nose, a bee on his knee, etc.

Runny Babbit by Shel Silverstein
Silverstein calls this a "billy sook," and this expression clearly relates to the text involved. Some main characters: Ploppy Sig, Pilly Belican, and Tot Jurtle.

The Hungry Thing by Jan Slepian and Ann Seidler
A hungry thing wants to be fed things like shmancakes and tickles. The townspeople have to figure out what it is he wants to eat.

Children's Poetry Books

We would be remiss if we did not include some of our favorite books of poetry in this section. Reading students rich and wonderful poetry is an excellent and natural way to develop phonemic awareness. The following is a list of our favorite poetry books. The publishing information for these books can be found in the Children's Literature Cited section.

- *Tomie dePaola's Mother Goose* by Tomie dePaola

- *Sing a Song of Popcorn* by de Regniers, Schenk, White, and Bennett

- *The Sky Is Full of Song* by Lee Bennett Hopkins

- *When the Dark Comes Dancing* by Nancy Larrick

- *The Helen Oxenbury Nursery Story Book* by Helen Oxenbury

- *The Random House Book of Poetry for Children* by Jack Prelutsky

- *Read Aloud Rhymes for the Very Young* by Jack Prelutsky

- *Something Big Has Been Here* by Jack Prelutsky

- *Where the Sidewalk Ends* by Shel Silverstein

Concluding Remarks

We cannot stress too heavily the importance of phonemic awareness to students' reading success. Stanovich (1986) has implied that phonemic awareness is the most important pedagogical breakthrough of this century. However, learning the sounds of our language is not enough to enhance reading success. Students must also have symbols to attach to these sounds. This will be discussed at length in the next chapter.

Important Points to Remember

- Phonemic awareness is the awareness that sounds are in our language and that spoken words are made up of individual sounds.

- The importance of phonemic awareness to reading success cannot be stressed too much.

- Students need to be trained in phonemic knowledge, but we suggest that teachers avoid word/sound drills and worksheets. What we are suggesting is language play—fully immersing children in rhymes, rhythms, word play, and rich, predictable literature.

- Reading poetry to students is an excellent and natural way to develop phonemic awareness.

Post-Reading Reflection

1. Review the seven steps in phonemic awareness training. What is one step that you can use to enrich your instruction in the classroom? Create two activities appropriate to your grade level that focus on this necessary step.

2. Which books or poems will you use to promote students' phonemic awareness?

Chapter 4

The Alphabet

As students gain an awareness of the sounds of our language, they need to become comfortable with the letters of the alphabet. Students need to recognize upper- and lowercase letters and recognize these letters in a rich variety of settings. Students will ultimately attach sounds to the letters of the alphabet as they engage in the process called phonics. As phonics is a sound/symbol activity, students' chances of success are greatly increased when both the sounds (phonemes) and symbols (alphabet) are familiar friends. Before we introduce how to teach the alphabet, we first present an assessment process for alphabet knowledge. Strategies for teaching the letters of the alphabet will follow. The chapter concludes with an excellent list of children's alphabet books to read to and share with students.

Assessing Knowledge of the Alphabet

We have developed a quick and easy assessment process to examine students' knowledge of the alphabet. The letters of the alphabet are placed in random order in two groups. The first group has the alphabet in lowercase letters and the second group has the alphabet in uppercase letters. The following is an example:

e b x	B X E
t n i	N I T
a f u	F U A
l j r	J R L
d h z	H Z D
v g q	G Q V
o w c	W C O
m k y	K Y M
p s	S P

The teacher should make one master copy for all students to examine and one copy per student on which to record student responses. Give the test to students individually. There are two steps to the process. First, ask a student to look at the master copy and say the name of each lower and uppercase letter. On the student's individual copy, mark a plus (+) if he or she gives the correct response. Put a check mark for an incorrect response to the right of the letter. If the student names all of the letters correctly, stop the assessment process at this point because this indicates that the student knows the letters of the alphabet. Second, if the student has difficulty, continue the assessment. Try saying the letters of the alphabet aloud in random order. Do this with both lower and uppercase letters. Mark a plus to the right of all letters that the student points to correctly. If the student cannot locate the letter, put a check to the right. If students are successful with this approach, they have a working knowledge of the alphabet but still need ongoing reinforcement and practice with the letters. If the student has difficulty with both components, you have identified the target letters for further instruction.

Once the assessment is finished and students' needs are determined, the instructional task becomes more efficient and effective.

Strategies for Developing Knowledge of the Alphabet

Adams supplies us with an important consideration when making decisions as to how to teach the alphabet. She says:

> The ability to name and recognize letters is, in general, not established through showing the children the letters and then teaching them the names. That's backwards. Most children are taught the letters only after they know their names. By thoroughly learning the names first, the child has a solid mnemonic peg to which the precept of the letter can be connected as it is built. By thoroughly teaching the names first, the teacher can methodically exploit them toward developing the child's sense of the functionally equivalent and distinctive differences between characters (Adams 1990, 359).

Toward this end, we suggest a variety of alphabet books to read to students on a regular basis so that they become familiar with the names of the alphabet letters. It is the rare student who does not enjoy Martin and Archambault's *Chicka Chicka Boom Boom* (2000). The pure joy of saying "A told B and B told C, I'll meet you at the top of the coconut tree," helps make the alphabet a well-known acquaintance rather than something to be feared. It is also important not to forget an old friend, "The Alphabet Song." This is something all students enjoy. Sing it on a consistent basis to make students comfortable with the names of the letters.

Once students know the names of the letters of the alphabet, the next step is to learn to recognize each letter and attach the name that they have already learned. To do this, we must decide on the appropriate order in which to teach the letters. Manzo and Manzo (1995) report there are four groups of letters that tend to produce confusion for students. Therefore, the following groups of letters should not be taught at the same time:

1. e, a, s, c, o

2. b, d, p, o, g, h

3. f, l, t, k, i, h

4. n, m, u, h, r

While this is important information to know, personal experience and the literature indicate that first teaching the letters of the alphabet that students find personally valuable is the most successful approach (Treiman and Boderick 1998). Students learn best, and often easiest, the letters of their own names. And, when a class has Bill, Brianna, Belinda, and Bernardo as members, it would seem remiss not to introduce the letter *B* and its name early in the instructional process. Students should begin writing words with the letters that they have learned as early as possible. However, having students copy or trace long lists of letters is not the answer. In regard to this, Adams supplies some important information. "Copying, of course, must be used; it is a necessary step toward the independent printing of a letter. But it appears that neither tracing nor copying, but independent printing holds the greatest leverage for perceptual and motor learning of letter shapes" (Adams 1990, 364). In short, teach students that they have important things to write and that knowing the alphabet allows them to write these important things. While Bradley and Jones (2007) state that there are relatively few empirical studies on how best to teach the alphabet, we have found the following activities effective in guiding students to know their letter names.

1. Take a photograph of each of your students. Print the pictures and place them in alphabetical order on a wall where the class can see them. Below each photo, print the letter each student's name begins with. If the names of multiple students start with the same letter, use last names to represent letters. If there are still too many students representing the same letter, have students adopt a stuffed animal that represents another letter. Not many classrooms have students whose first or last name starts with the letter Z. Instead, find a stuffed zebra and take the student's picture with the zebra. Place this photograph on the wall and print the letter Z below the picture. Students then become the class experts on the letters placed with their photos. If students have difficulty with the name of a letter, they can look at the pictures on the wall and seek help from the student whose name begins with the letter that they find challenging.

2. At the beginning of the year, sing the alphabet song whenever you have the opportunity. This can be while students are standing in line waiting to come in from recess or as you move from one literacy activity to another.

3. Place the letters of the alphabet on which you are focusing around the exit doors of your classroom. Have students each point to a letter and name it as they leave the room.

4. Place the letters of the alphabet at eye level around the classroom. When students finish other activities, they can take an alphabet walk in pairs. Give each pair of students a flashlight. When one student in the pair says a letter name correctly, have the other student turn on the flashlight and shine it on the correctly named letter.

5. Read children's literature that features a main character or activity that begins with the letter being studied. Peet's (1984) *Big Bad Bruce* or *Lilly's Purple Plastic Purse* by Henkes (1996) are naturals.

6. Have several alphabet books available for students during sustained silent reading time or during free time.

7. Provide ample opportunity for students to write. Every time students write letters, they become more and more familiar with that letter.

8. Read Tryon's *Albert's Alphabet* (1991), and then take an alphabet walk around the school yard looking for objects that start with the letters of the alphabet the class is learning.

9. Make an alphabet tree so that when letters are learned, they are printed on cutout leaves and placed on the tree. Letters can be both upper and lower case. A coconut tree is ideal, especially after reading Martin and Archambault's *Chicka Chicka Boom Boom* (2000).

10. Read *My Name is Alice* (Bayer 1992). Create a class alphabet book. Change the dialogue from, "A, my name is Alice and my husband's name is Alex. We come from Alaska and we see ants," to "A, my name is Andy and I like apples." You can have more than one student on a page to represent a letter or more than one page to represent a letter. If there are various letters of the alphabet not represented by students' names, school teachers, aides, and specialists whose names begin with the appropriate letter can be interviewed. Each page should be illustrated.

Alphabet Books

Earlier, we mentioned reading alphabet books to students. The following is a list of our favorite choices. For a more comprehensive selection, we suggest examining Chaney's (1993) *Alphabet Books: Resources for Learning*. The publishing information for the books listed below can be found in the Children's Literature Cited section.

- *Anno's Alphabet* by Mitsumasa Anno

- *Animalia* by Graeme Base

- *My Name is Alice* by Jane Bayer

- *Alphabet Out Loud* by R. G. Bragg

- *ABC Discovery!* by Izhar Cohen

- *Eating the Alphabet: Fruits and Vegetables from A to Z* by Lois Ehlert

- *Alphabet Under Construction* by Denise Fleming

- *26 Letters and 99 Cents* by Tana Hoban

- *Animal Alphabet* by Bert Kitchen

- *Achoo! Bang! The Noisy Alphabet* by Ross MacDonald

- *Chicka Chicka Boom Boom* by Bill Martin Jr. and John Archambault

- *Albert's Alphabet* by Leslie Tryon

- *The Z Was Zapped* by Chris Van Allsburg

- *The Alphabet from Z to A (With much confusion on the way)* by Judith Viorst

- *New Alphabet of Animals* by Christopher Wormell

- *All in the Woodland Early: An ABC Book* by Jane Yolen

Concluding Remarks

At this point, students should have a firm knowledge of the alphabet. Also, they should be aware of the sounds of our language. Then it is time for them to become aware of the alphabetic principle—to realize that the alphabet letters not only have names but they also have sounds. Once students realize this, they need a variety of opportunities to write. Do not hesitate to encourage invented spelling. Invented spelling is an excellent indicator that students are aware of the alphabetic principle and are beginning to see the relationship between the sounds in our language and the letters of the alphabet. When this occurs, students are generally ready to formally begin learning phonics.

Important Points to Remember

- As students gain an awareness of the sounds of our language, they need to become comfortable with the letters of the alphabet.

- Students should begin writing words with the letters they have learned as early as possible.

- Invented spelling is an excellent indicator that students are phonemically aware and are often ready to formally begin learning phonics.

Post-Reading Reflection

1. Why do you think it is important to assess letter knowledge?

2. How will you teach letters that are personally important to your students? Try looking at your class roster for clusters of names with common initial letters.

3. Did you learn about any new alphabet books in this chapter? Choose three alphabet books that you plan to share with your class.

Chapter 5

. . . .
Phonics
. . . .

W**e are going to begin by making an unusual statement—phonics does not work very well.** Now that we have your attention, it seems important to state that while phonics does not work very well, it is still a useful and important tool in a young reader's toolbox of word analysis options. How can we say that phonics does not work well and yet maintain that it is an important word analysis tool? We will begin by discussing why it does not always work well.

In *The Mother Tongue: English and How It Got That Way*, Bryson explains:

> In some languages, such as Finnish, there is a neat one-to-one correspondence between sound and spelling. A *k* to the Finns is always /k/, and *l* is eternally and comfortingly /l/. But in English, pronunciation is so various—one might say random—that not one of the 26 letters can be relied on for constancy. Either the letters have a variety of pronunciations, as with the *c* in *race*, *rack*, and *rich*, or they sulk in silence, like the *b*

in *debt*, the *a* in *bread*, and the second *t* in *thistle*. In combinations, they become even more unruly and unpredictable, most famously in the letter cluster *ough*, which can be pronounced in any of eight ways—as in *through, though, thought, tough, plough, thorough, hiccough,* and *lough* (an English word for *lake* or *loch*, pronounced roughly as the latter). The pronunciation possibilities are so various that probably not one English speaker in a hundred could pronounce with confidence the name of a crow-like bird called a *chough*. (It's chuff.) Two words in English, *hegemony* and *phthisis*, have nine pronunciations each. But perhaps nothing speaks more clearly for the absurdities of English pronunciation than the word for the study of pronunciation in English, *orthoepy*, which can be pronounced two ways (1990, 85).

In *Beginning to Read: Thinking and Learning About Print*, Adams states, "As material to be taught or learned, individual letter-sound correspondence and phonic generalizations are inherently intractable when divorced from the rest of the reading situation. They are abstract, piecemeal, unorderable, unreliable, barely numerable, and sometimes mutually incompatible" (Adams 1990, 291). Why would Adams, a supporter of explicitly teaching phonics, make such a statement? Let us examine the word *phonics* from a sound-symbol perspective and the word from left to right, as many young readers would. We will do this in a question-and-answer format.

What sound does the first letter of phonics *make?*

Unfortunately, the *p* does not make a sound in the word *phonics*.

What sound does the h *make?*

It, like the *p*, does not make a sound in the word *phonics*.

Can the p *and* h *be put together?*

Yes, but when put together, neither the sound of *p* nor the sound of *h* is heard. Instead, the /f/ sound is heard.

What sound does the vowel o make? Does it make the long vowel sound, as heard in oak, *or the short vowel sound, as heard in* hot?

It makes the short vowel sound as heard in *hot*. However, it is not an easy sound to distinguish in the middle of a word such as *phonics*.

What sound does the letter c *make? Does it ever have its own sound like we think of most consonants having?*

It does not have its own sound. Instead, it produces either the /k/ or the /s/ sound. In the word *phonics*, the *c* produces the /k/ sound.

As you see, the sound-symbol process is not a perfect one, not even with an important word like *phonics*, the name of the process. Now, try to associate sounds with the symbols (letters) of much more interesting words. To most adults, and certainly to students, names are very important. And, as names come from a variety of different cultures and different languages, the sounds traditionally associated with symbols often just do not work. Stop reading this text for a moment and give phonics a try with your own name or, if you teach, the names on your class roster.

If you paused while trying to use phonics with your name, you probably agree with our initial statement that phonics does not always work well. If so, how can it also be stated that phonics is an important decoding tool? The rest of this chapter will supply an answer.

While phonics does not work as well as we would like, it works well enough to assist students as they seek meaning. However, phonics is just one component of the reading process. Producing students who can use the sound-symbol process, while important, is not sufficient for producing good readers. This chapter addresses all aspects of phonics. It starts with a brief history.

A Brief History

Phonic skills—should we or should we not teach them? And if we should teach them, how should they be taught? These are not new questions. In fact, they have been asked since children were first taught to read. The debate over teaching phonics has been long and often acrimonious. Beginning in the Middle Ages, when the first primers were introduced, the teaching of reading generally followed a part-to-whole process. The alphabet was taught first, followed by sounds (often using target words), and then syllables and short words. This practice continued well into the 1800s. However, in 1840, the pendulum began to shift toward the whole-word method, and the debate became heated.

According to Smith, *My Little Primer*, written in 1840 by Josiah Bumstead, was the first reader to be based specifically on the look-say method. Bumstead expressed the justification for his method as follows:

> In teaching reading, the general practice has been to begin with the alphabet, and drill the child upon the letters, month after month, until he is supposed to have acquired them. This method, so irksome and vexatious to both teacher and scholar, is now giving place to another, which experience has proven to be more philosophical, intelligent, pleasant, and rapid. It is that of beginning with familiar and easy words, instead of letters (Smith 1967).

Bumstead presented his case gently in comparison to Horace Mann. Horace Mann, an early advocate of public school education, became disenchanted with phonics and stressed that students be taught rich, meaningful words rather than letters, those "skeleton-shaped, bloodless, ghostly apparitions" (Balmuth 1982, 190). Gradually, the influence of a whole-word approach grew and received its most encouraging support in 1908, when Huey, in *The Psychology and Pedagogy of Reading*, reported on research that he had conducted. Huey found that, when adults looked at individual letters and then four-, eight-, and twelve-letter words, the multiplication of letters made proportionately little difference in the ease or speed of recognition. Based on this evidence, he argued that words must be read as a whole and not letter by letter. Huey's research added ammunition to whole-word advocates and their approach began to take hold during the second quarter of that century. During the first half of the century, William S. Gray, the first president of the International Reading Association and who is often referred to as "the father of Dick and Jane," introduced a basal series that he may have considered to be a balance between phonics and a whole-word approach. However, Gray would be the first to admit that he was not a fan of using explicit phonic instruction, and his basal series personified the look-say approach that dominated instruction through the early 1950s. In 1955, the pendulum swing toward whole-word instruction slowed.

In 1955, *Why Johnny Can't Read* was published. The author, Rudolph Flesch, appealed, if not to our common sense, then at least to our sense of patriotism: "There is a connection between phonics and democracy—a fundamental connection. Equal opportunity for all is one of the inalienable rights, and the word method interferes with that right" (Flesch 1955, 130). While the logic of this statement is certainly weak, his impact on the general public was not. *Why Johnny Can't Read* was on most best seller lists for more than 30 weeks. A close reading of *Why Johnny Can't Read* reveals an often simplistic view of the reading process. However, the book was a significant step in polarizing educators' thoughts about the phonics/whole-word debate. In the mid-1960s, two important individuals in the field of reading, through their research and writing, took the debate to a higher level.

In 1967, Jeanne Chall's *Learning to Read: The Great Debate* clearly stated that a synthetic (explicitly taught phonics) approach is superior to an analytical (whole-word) approach. Chall reviewed the significant research that had been conducted from 1910 to 1965 and came to the conclusion that systematic, explicit phonic instruction is an important component of beginning reading instruction. Interestingly, also in 1967, Kenneth Goodman, certainly the individual most responsible for the whole-language movement, presented a paper and later published an article titled *Reading: A Psycholinguistic Guessing Game* (1972). In this article, Goodman laid the groundwork for the concept that reading is a top-down, meaning-centered approach, where phonics is learned implicitly by students immersed in the reading and writing process. He also asserted that systematic phonic instruction is not an important component of early reading instruction. Intentionally or not, Chall and Goodman intensified the confusion and conflict regarding the function of phonics in beginning reading instruction. Over the next 20 years, the concept of reading as a top-down process, as supported by Goodman, had the greatest influence on early reading instruction. This began to change in 1985.

Becoming a Nation of Readers: The Report of the Commission on Reading was published in 1985. This report clearly supported the concept that reading must be meaning-centered. However, after much of the significant research on beginning reading instruction had been investigated, the commission made the following strong statement in *Becoming a Nation of Readers*: "The issue is no longer, as it was several decades ago, whether children should be taught phonics. The issues now are specific ones of just how it should be done" (Anderson et al. 1985, 37). The question "How should it be done?" was answered this way, "When the criterion is children's year-to-year gains on standardized reading achievement tests, the available research does not permit a decisive answer, although the trend of the data favors explicit phonics" (Anderson et al. 1985, 42). While *Becoming a Nation of Readers* added support to Chall's suppositions in *Learning to Read: The Great Debate*, with its statement that children must be taught phonics, the answer to how it should be taught, explicitly or implicitly, was much weaker. In 1990, stronger support to Chall's stance on the great debate was provided.

Beginning to Read: Thinking and Learning About Print was written in conjunction with the Reading Research Center at the Center for the Study of Reading at the University of Illinois (Adams 1990). It was supported by the Office of Educational Research and Improvement (OERI) of the United States Department of Education. Author Marilyn Jager Adams provided a comprehensive look at the research on beginning reading instruction and then took a significant step in concluding the phonics debate. She stated, in fact insisted, that the teaching of beginning reading must involve phonics taught systematically and early. Adams's book is an impressive document. It carefully examines the debate about phonics, and it is persuasive in its conclusions. *Beginning to Read* is a difficult book to ignore. Further support for the systematic teaching of phonics came from the National Reading Panel (2000). In 1997, Congress asked the Director of the National Institute of Child Health and Human Development (NICHD) at the National Institutes of Health, in consultation with the Secretary of Education, to convene a national panel to assess the effectiveness of different approaches used to teach children to read. Reviewing and analyzing more than 100,000 studies on reading, The National Reading Panel found five components essential to a child's learning to read: phonemic awareness, phonics, vocabulary, fluency, and comprehension. Of particular importance to this text, The National Reading Panel, after examining research related to the teaching of phonics, concluded that explicit, systematic phonic instruction is more effective than hit-or-miss instruction or no instruction at all. *Reading First*, the academic heart of the No Child Left Behind Act (2002), grew out of the findings of the National Reading

Panel and correspondingly stresses the importance of explicit, systematic phonic instruction.

So, for the moment, "The Great Debate," as Chall described it, has been settled. Beginning in 1985, with the publication of *Becoming a Nation of Readers*, the pendulum has swung firmly toward accepting phonics as a significant component of beginning reading instruction and to viewing systematic phonic instruction as a viable, and perhaps preferable, instructional strategy.

An Important Consideration

Teaching students to use phonic skills should be a part of reading instruction; however, how the skills are taught continues to be a point of concern. While the evidence leans toward teaching phonics explicitly, it is far from overwhelming. Let us reexamine the statement, "When the criterion is children's year-to-year gains on standardized reading achievement tests, the available research does not permit a decisive answer, although the trend of the data favors explicit phonics" (Anderson et al. 1985, 42). For additional consideration, couple such a statement with the following made by Chall in *Learning to Read: The Great Debate*.

> A beginning code-emphasis program will not cure all reading ills. It cannot guarantee that *all* children will learn to read easily. Nor have the results of meaning-emphasis programs been so disastrous that all academic and emotional failures can be blamed on them, as some proponents and publishers of new code-emphasis programs claim. But the evidence does show that a changeover to code-emphasis programs for the beginner can improve the situation somewhat, and in this all too imperfect world even a small improvement is worth working for. I believe that method changes, if made in the right spirit, will lead to improved reading standards (Chall 1967, 309).

These statements, while supportive of the explicit teaching of phonics, are certainly not overwhelmingly powerful endorsements.

While Adams is firm in her commitment to explicit phonic instruction, she is not supportive of a bottom-up approach—the approach most often associated with explicit phonic instruction, where one skill must sequentially follow another. She makes this statement when discussing effective reading programs:

> Finally, none of these programs embodies the misguided hypothesis that reading skills are best developed from the bottom up. In the reading situation, as in any effective communication situation, the message or text provides but one of the critical sources of information. The rest must come from readers' own prior knowledge. Further, in the reading situation as in any other learning situation, the learnability of a pattern depends critically on the prior knowledge and higher-order relationships it evokes. In both fluent reading and its acquisition, the reader's knowledge must be aroused interactively and in parallel. Neither understanding nor learning can proceed hierarchically from the bottom up. Phonological awareness, letter recognition facility, familiarity with spelling patterns, spelling-sound relations, and individual words must be developed in concert with real reading and real writing and with deliberate reflection on the forms, functions, and meanings of texts (Adams 1990, 422).

What seems important to remember, as one examines the history of this great debate, is that the reading needs of students are more important than winning the debate. There seems to be strong agreement that phonics should be taught. There is less agreement as to how it should be taught. If there continues to be a debate, it is on how best to teach this central component of the word analysis process. It is our contention that there is no one best way to teach phonics, but we stress that it be taught in meaningful ways. What is important is that teachers know the skills of phonics backward and forward, know their students' skill needs, and guide students to see the importance of the skills being taught.

A Definition and Overview

As defined earlier, phonics is the association of sounds with symbols. Because our alphabet consists of consonants and vowels, phonics is the process of giving sounds to the letters of the alphabet. This seems like a straightforward process. However, associating sounds with the letters of the alphabet can be a challenging process. Differences abound, depending on where one lives, the dialect used in that region, and the words that one is trying to read. In California, people put *oil* in their cars, while in Texas, *all* is added. Speaking of *car*, where does the *r* go when it is pronounced in and around New York City? What is important to remember is that the sound-symbol relationship varies from word to word, from person to person, and from region to region. The authors of *Becoming a Nation of Readers* make this statement: "All that phonics can be expected to do is help children get approximate pronunciations" (Anderson et al. 1985, 41). As each of us has developed a different process for the use of phonics, we need to guide our students to develop the concept that phonics is not a perfect process but one that needs to be personalized. When students realize this, they are on their way to developing their own logic of the code. For this to happen, students must be taught the most essential components of phonics very early in their reading careers. In *Becoming a Nation of Readers*, the task is stated clearly, "The right maxims for phonics are: Do it early. Keep it simple" (Anderson et al. 1985, 43).

To follow this statement, we will examine three areas. We will define important terms associated with phonics, look at significant sound-symbol relationships, and examine the phonic generalizations, or rules, that do and do not work.

Phonic Terms

The following terms are commonly used in relation to phonics. The definitions are ours but, in almost all cases, closely reflect common definitions found in professional literature.

Vowels

The letters *a, e, i, o,* and *u* are always labeled vowels. The letters *y* and *w* sometimes function as vowels when at the end of words. The vowel sound is one produced by a relatively free passage of the air stream through the voice-making mechanisms.

Consonants

Consonants are usually those letters that are not vowels. The consonant sound is one produced by a partial or complete obstruction of the air stream through the voice-making mechanisms. Again, the letters *y* and *w* can cause confusion. They are normally consonants at the beginnings of words and vowels at the end of words.

Consonant Digraphs

A consonant digraph is two consecutive consonants representing one sound. There are both regular and variant digraphs. Regular digraphs produce a single sound, unique to the two consonants involved. The *ch* in *chin* is a regular digraph.

Variant digraphs produce a sound associated with an existing letter of the alphabet. The *ph* in *phonics*, the *gh* in *enough*, and the *ch* in *character* are variant digraphs. Most digraphs, both regular and variant, have the letter *h* as the second of the two letters involved. The *ng* at the end of words, such as *thing*, is the exception.

Phonic Terms *(cont.)*

Consonant Blends

A consonant blend is two or more consecutive consonants that work or blend together while maintaining their own sounds. The *str* in *street* is an example of a blend, as is the *fl* in *flower*. Consonant blends are sometimes labeled consonant clusters.

Hard C

The letter *c* generally produces the /k/ sound when followed by *a, o, u,* or a consonant.

Soft C

The letter *c* generally produces the /s/ sound when followed by *e, i,* or *y*.

Hard G

The letter *g* generally produces a /g/ sound when followed by *a, o, u,* or a consonant.

Soft G

The letter *g* generally produces the /j/ sound when followed by *e, i,* or *y*.

Long Vowels

It is generally stated that long vowels say their own name. The *a* in *ape* would be labeled a long vowel sound. Long vowels are sometimes called glided vowels.

Short Vowels

Short vowel sounds, sometimes called unglided vowels, are the phonemes associated with the vowels in the words *at, egg, it, ox,* and *bum*.

Phonic Terms *(cont.)*

R-Controlled Vowels

When a vowel is followed by an *r*, the vowel is generally neither long nor short but influenced by the *r*. The word *car* is a good example of an *r*-controlled vowel.

Vowel Diphthongs

Diphthongs are tricky concepts. *Diphthong* is a Greek word that means "having two sounds." While the term *diphthong* can be applied to both consonants and vowels, in reading we generally talk about vowel diphthongs. A vowel diphthong is a subtle combination of two vowel sounds. The vowel combinations most often labeled as diphthongs are the *oi* in *oil*, *oy* in *toy*, *ow* in *cow*, and *ou* in *out*.

Vowel Digraphs

Vowel digraphs are generally defined as two consecutive vowels producing one sound. There are regular and variant forms. Regular vowel digraphs produce sounds that are long, as in the word *bead*, and variant vowel digraphs produce sounds that are not long, as in the word *bread*. The concept of regular as long and variant as not long offers students little useful information. From the students' perspective, when they see two consecutive vowels, they know the combination may produce a single long or not long sound unless, of course, they are dealing with a diphthong or an *oo* combination.

Schwa

The schwa is neither a long nor a short sound. It is the sound heard in the initial letter *a* of the word *afraid*. It is typically found in the unaccented syllable of words.

Sound/Symbol Relationships

Consonant Sounds

b	bear	j	jug	q	queen	x	box
c	cat	k	king	r	race	y	yellow
d	dog	l	lake	s	seven	z	zebra
f	face	m	monkey	t	teacher		
g	goat	n	nice	v	vase		
h	hen	p	pear	w	wagon		

Vowel Sounds

Short Sounds		Long Sounds		Vowel + r
a	at	a	ace	far
e	echo	e	equal	her
i	it	i	ice	dirt
o	ox	o	open	more
u	up	u	unicorn	fur

Consonants with Two or More Sounds

c	g	s	x
consonant	got	six	xylophone
city	gyrate	is	exist
		sure	box

58

Sound/Symbol Relationships *(cont.)*

Consonant Blends (Beginning of words)

bl	blend	gl	glue	sn	snail
br	bright	gr	grumpy	sp	spot
cl	clear	pl	place	spl	splash
cr	crown	scr	screech	spr	spring
dr	drive	shr	shrink	st	stop
dw	dwell	sk	sky	str	street
fl	floor	sl	slippery	sw	swim
fr	from	sm	smell	thr	through

Consonant Blends (End of Words)

ld	child	nd	send	rd	word
mp	camp	nt	bent	sk	risk

Consonant Digraphs

(Regular)				(Variant)			
ch	church	th	that	ch	character	ph	phone
sh	ship	wh	when	gh	enough		

Diphthongs

oi	oil	ou	out	ow	cow	oy	toy

If the previous information sounds precise and consistent, it is important to remember that we are dealing with an imperfect system. Bryson (1990) tells us that we have more than 40 sounds in English and over 200 ways of spelling them. We can render the *sh* in up to 14 ways; we can spell the long *o* and long *a* in more than a dozen ways. If we count proper nouns, the word *air* can be spelled in a remarkable 38 ways. We must be especially careful and consistent as we select the phonic rules or generalizations to teach students so they can be as successful as possible.

Phonic Rules

Roe, Smith, and Burns (2005) felt that students should not be inundated with rules. They examined the lists of generalizations by Bailey (1967), Burmeister (1968), Clymer (1963), and Evans (1967) and concluded that out of the multitude of rules that could be taught, the following list was sufficiently short and useful.

1. When the letters *c* and *g* are followed by *e, i,* or *y,* they generally have soft sounds: the /s/ sound for the letter *c* and the /j/ sound for the letter *g*. (Examples are *cent, city,* and *giant.*) When *c* and *g* are followed by *o, a,* or *u,* they generally have hard sounds: *g* has its own sound, and *c* has the sound of /k/. (Examples are *cat, cut,* and *go.*)

2. When any two like consonants are next to each other, only one is sounded, as in *letter* and *butter*.

3. The letters *ch* usually have the sound heard in *church,* although it sometimes sounds like /sh/ or /k/ as in *Charlotte* and *character.*

4. When *kn* are the first two letters in a word, the *k* is not sounded, as in *knot*.

5. When *wr* are the first two letters in a word, the *w* is not sounded, as in *write*.

6. When *ck* are the last two letters in a word, the sound of the letter *k* is given, as in *truck*.

7. The sound of a vowel preceding *r* is neither long nor short, as in *car* and *far*.

8. In the vowel combinations *oa, ee, ai*, and *ay*, the first vowel is generally long and the second is not sounded, as in *boat*.

9. The double vowels *oi, oy*, and *ou* usually form diphthongs. The *ow* combination frequently stands for the long *o* sound, but it may also form a diphthong (e.g., *toy, out*, and *cow*).

10. If a word has one vowel and that vowel is at the end of the word, the vowel usually represents its long sound, as in *go*.

11. If a word has only one vowel and the vowel is not at the end of the word, the vowel usually represents its short sound, as in *cat*.

12. If a word has two vowels and one is the final *e*, the first vowel is usually long and the final *e* is not sounded, as in *cake*.

Roe, Smith, and Burns (2005) stress that students must be guided to see that generalizations help them derive probable pronunciations rather than infallible results.

Strategies for Developing Phonic Skills

Before a discussion on strategies for teaching phonic skills can be initiated, a decision needs to be made on the order in which the components of phonics should be taught. The following information presents the order in which we suggest the concepts be taught and then provide a justification for our choice.

1. Begin with the consonant sounds /b/, hard *c* (/k/), /d/, hard /g/, /h/, /j/, /k/, /m/, /n/, /p/, /t/, and /w/.

    We suggest these consonants first as they are the most

consistent. They generally represent one sound. Within these consonants, we suggest teachers do not teach the sounds of letters *b, d,* and *p* at the same time because the sounds and letter shapes are similar and can be confused. The same is true of *m* and *n*. Teachers should also note that the letters *c, g, h,* and *w* can be more difficult to learn because their letter names are distinctively different from their sounds.

2. Teach the short sounds of the five common vowels /a/, /e/, /i/, /o/, and /u/.

    It is our experience that students find learning the short vowel sounds most useful. They can blend them with the consonants mentioned in the previous step to read a large number of one-syllable words.

3. Teach students the consonant sounds /f/, /l/, /r/, and /s/.

    We suggest waiting to teach these consonant sounds until students are comfortable with the more consistent consonants. Young students often find these sounds difficult to articulate.

4. Teach the soft *c* (/s/) and the soft *g* (/j/).

    It is a good idea to separate the teaching of the hard and soft *c* and *g* sounds to avoid confusing students. Let students get comfortable with the hard sounds and then teach them the soft sounds.

5. Teach the long sounds of the five common vowels.

    Again, let students get comfortable with the short vowel sounds and then teach them the long vowel sounds.

6. Teach appropriate rimes and corresponding onsets.

    Examine the rimes presented on page 80. Select those that include just the vowel and consonant sounds already introduced (i.e., the rime *at*, and the onsets of letters *b, c,* and *f*). Rimes are especially useful as they help students recognize familiar letter patterns and how the combinations influence the sounds that are made.

7. Teach the consonant sounds of the letters *q, v, x, y,* and *z.*

    We suggest waiting to teach the sounds associated with these consonants because they are not consistent. The *q* represents a new concept because it always works with the letter *u.* We also strongly suggest that *x* be taught in the final position of words such as *box* to avoid confusing students.

8. Teach the vowel + *r* generalization.

    Teach this after students become comfortable with the long and short sounds of the vowels.

9. Teach common two-letter consonant blends.

    Teach blends after students have mastered the individual consonant sounds.

10. Teach the consonant digraphs.

    Since the majority of consonant digraphs create single new sounds, do not introduce digraphs until after students have gained confidence in the sound/symbol process.

11. Teach the vowel diphthongs.

    Teach the vowel diphthongs *oi, oy, ou,* and *ow* after students have mastered the short and long vowel sounds.

12. Teach common three-letter consonant blends.

    The concepts of the blending of three consonants can often be a complex concept and a difficult task for young learners. There should be no hurry to teach them.

13. Teach other sound-symbol relationships on an as-needed basis.

We feel that the sound-symbol relationships that are not discussed in the previous list are either too rare or inconsistent to teach to students on a systematic basis. While many will argue with this, we feel that vowel digraphs and other, even more esoteric generalizations, are too confusing for many young readers. Students learning sound-symbol relationships are often hindered rather than helped by trying to learn the difference between such concepts as the voiced and unvoiced /th/. In *Becoming a Nation of Readers*, the authors stated clearly, "The right maxims for phonics are: Do it early. Keep it simple" (Anderson et al. 1985, 43). Manzo and Manzo are even more basic: "A little bit of phonics can go a long way" (1995, 187).

We have presented the order in which we like to teach phonic concepts. The next step is developing a process for teaching phonic skills. Cunningham, Moore, and Cunningham (1989) have developed a seven-step prototype for a phonic lesson that we particularly like. The steps are listed below, and are followed by a sample lesson.

1. Review and explain the goal of the lesson.

2. Teach auditory discrimination of the sound.

3. Teach association of the letter with sound by using a known word as a key word.

4. Have students find the letter in other words and remind them that letters do not always have the same sounds.

5. Have students apply the sound while figuring out new words during the lesson.

6. Guide students in applying their new letter-sound knowledge to reading.

7. Remind students to apply the sound when reading on their own.

The following is an example of a phonic lesson that uses

these seven steps with some modification. Step three is a key component of the lesson. We have found that when students can take the sound being taught and relate it to words that are already in their speaking vocabularies, the sound becomes much less abstract and more real to them. In this lesson, we focus on the /p/ sound.

1. "Today we are going to learn another consonant sound. Do you remember the sound for the consonant *n*? Do you remember the key word for this sound?" Write *nifty* and *n* on the board to help students remember. "Today, we will learn the consonant sound for the letter *p* and come up with a key word for the sound."

2. "The /p/ sound is the sound we hear at the beginning of Pierre's name. I hear the sound /p/ at the beginning of these words: *puppy, pencil,* and *paper*. I am going to say some more words. Listen to see if the words begin with the same sound as *Pierre*. If they do, make a smile on your face. If they do not, make a frown." Say the words *Petunia, pal, art, Ralph,* and *etch*. Watch for students' responses. Continue until you are sure students are comfortable hearing the difference between the /p/ sound and other beginning consonant sounds.

3. "I have said a lot of words that begin with the /p/ sound. I want you to pick the word that you think best makes that sound. The word can have the sound at its beginning, middle, or end." Have students nominate words and tell why they like them. Write their suggestions on the board. Have the class vote on the word that they think is the best key word. Have the student whose word is selected wear a card for the rest of the day with the word printed on it and the *p* underlined. Designate him or her the "P Sound Expert" for the day.

4. "Remember yesterday I read you a story called *Lilly's Purple Plastic Purse* (Henkes 1996)? I am going to read it again. Listen and see if you hear the /p/ sound in some of the words in the story." Read the story to students and slightly emphasize words with the /p/ sound. "Now, I am going to write its title on the board." Write the title on the board. "Who can come up and underline the letter *p*?" Once each letter is underlined, have students decide if the underlined letter has the same sound as the chosen key word. Remind students that the letter *p* can sometimes be found in the middle or at the end of words.

5. Write the word *pen* on the board. Ask students what sound the letter *n* makes and explain that the *e* makes the short *e* sound. Place your hand under the *p* and have them say the sound. Place your hand under the *e* and you say the sound, then under the *n* and have them say the sound. "Now I am going to say the same sounds and blend them all together. What is the word I am saying when the sounds are blended together?"

6. "Now we are going to read a story that has some new words with the letter *p*. When you see these words, try to find the /p/ sound that you hear in our key word. Remember, the *p* will sometimes be in the middle or at the end of words. Try the sound and see if you can come up with a word that makes sense in the story." Read the story until you come to a word with a /p/ sound. Guide students through sounding out the word. Do this until students are comfortable with the process. Then let them read on their own.

7. "We have learned a new sound today. What is it?" Ask students what the key word is for the sound. "When we see a word with the letter *p* in it, it will almost always make the /p/ sound we hear in the key word. As you are reading today, see if you can use the /p/ sound to help you read new words."

8. At the next break or when students have the opportunity to leave the room, stand by the door holding a purple plastic

purse. Tell the students that to leave the room, they will need to place something in the purse that begins with the /p/ sound. If you spot a student picking up a sheet of paper, a pencil, or perhaps a pink eraser, call on him or her to come up and place it in the purse and ask the other students if it begins with the /p/ sound. If you cannot find a purple plastic purse, color a lunch bag purple, staple on a handle made out of a paper strip, and use it as a substitute.

9. When students return, or during the next language arts period, review the /p/ sound, the target word selected, and the story *Lilly's Purple Plastic Purse*. Write the following prompt on the board, "In Lilly's purple, plastic purse I will put a _____." Review what might be placed in the purse and write the words on the board. Then have each student write the prompt on his or her own and an object that he or she would place in the purse. Having students write the letter *p* several times is excellent reinforcement of the letter and its sound.

Students do not seem to tire of variations of this process. Whenever possible, enrich this process by giving students the opportunity to write for a variety of purposes. It is important that invented spelling be supported. As students use invented spelling, they are thinking about the sounds that represent letters. This can be a very powerful process for students to gain insight and to reinforce sound-symbol relationships.

Children's Books That Feature Specific Sounds

We have featured good children's literature for every component of the word analysis process. This section on phonics is no different. As a sound is introduced, read literature that features that sound to students. This introduces students to two important concepts. First, good literature brims with familiar sounds. Second, students who learn their sound-symbol relationships will eventually be able to read many of the exciting books that have been read to them. The following list features books that represent important sounds. The publishing information for these books can be found in the Children's Literature Cited section.

Short *a*

Anno's Alphabet by Mitsumasa Anno

Angus and the Cat by Marjorie Flack

Millions of Cats by Wanda Gag

Alex and the Cat by Hellen Griffith

There's an Ant in Anthony by Bernard Most

Who Took the Farmer's Hat? by Joan Nodset

The Gingerbread Man by Karen Schmidt

The Cat in the Hat by Dr. Seuss

The Cat in the Hat Comes Back by Dr. Seuss

Long *a*

The Paper Crane by Molly Bang

Katy and the Big Snow by Virginia Lee Burton

Sheila Rae, the Brave by Kevin Henkes

Short and Long *a*

Jack and Jake by Aliki

Caps for Sale by Esphyr Slobodkina

Short *e*

The Little Red Hen by Paul Galdone

Long *e*

Have You Seen Trees? by Joanne Oppenheim

The Sheep Follow by Monica Wellington

Short *i*

Willy the Wimp by Anthony Browne

Gilberto and the Wind Marie Hall Ets

Whistle for Willie by Ezra Jack Keats

Swimmy by Leo Lionni

Small Pig by Arnold Lobel

Long *i*

The Bike Lesson by Stan and Jan Berenstain

I Like Me by Nancy Carlson

When the Tide Is Low by Sheila Cole

Mike's Kite by Elizabeth MacDonald

Ira Sleeps Over by Bernard Waber

Short *o*

Oscar Otter by Nathaniel Benchley

Ten Black Dots by Donald Crews

Mogwogs on the March by Olivier Dunrea

Flossie and the Fox by Patricia C. McKissack

Fox in Socks by Dr. Seuss

Hop on Pop by Dr. Seuss

Long *o*

Roll Over! by Mordicai Gerstein

The Adventures of Mole and Troll by Tony Johnston

Night Noises and Other Mole and Troll Stories by Tony Johnston

Oh, A Hunting We Will Go by John Langstaff

Short *u*

Where's the Bunny? by Ruth Carroll

Umbrella Parade by Kathy Feczko

The Cut-Ups by James Marshall

Thump and Plunk by Janice M. Udry

Umbrella by Taro Yashima

Long *u*

Sarah's Unicorn by Bruce and Katharine Correlle

Tell Me a Trudy by Lore Segal

Letter B

Goldilocks and the Three Bears by Jan Brett

Best Friends by Miriam Cohen

Brown Bear, Brown Bear, What Do You See? by Bill Martin Jr.

Letter C

A Pocket for Corduroy by Don Freeman

Millions of Cats by Wanda Gag

Curious George by H. A. Rey

Letter D

Dinosaurs, Dragonflies, and Diamonds by Gail Gibbons

Make Way for Ducklings by Robert McCloskey

Letter F

Frederick by Leo Lionni

Friends by Helen Oxenbury

A Fish Out of Water by Helen Palmer

The Rainbow Fish by Marcus Pfister

Letter G

Goodnight Moon by Margaret Wise Brown

The Grouchy Ladybug by Eric Carle

Letter H

Building a House by Byron Barton

A House Is a House for Me by Mary Ann Hoberman

Houses and Homes by Ann Morris

Letter *J*

No Jumping on the Bed by Tedd Arnold

Hop, Jump by Ellen Stoll Walsh

Letter *K*

Katy No-Pocket by Emmy Payne

Momo's Kitten by Mitsu Yashima

Letter *L*

Lyle, Lyle, Crocodile by Bernard Waber

Letter *M*

Goodnight Moon by Margaret Wise Brown

Wait Till the Moon Is Full by Margaret Wise Brown

If You Give a Moose a Muffin by Laura Joffe Numeroff

If You Take a Mouse to the Movies by Laura Joffe Numeroff

Letter *N*

No Jumping on the Bed by Tedd Arnold

There's Something in My Attic by Mercer Mayer

The Napping House by Audrey Wood

Letter *P*

Pancakes, Pancakes by Eric Carle

Lilly's Purple Plastic Purse by Kevin Henkes

Little Pink Pig by Pat Hutchins

If You Give a Pig a Pancake by Laura Joffe Numeroff

If You Give a Pig a Party by Laura Joffe Numeroff

It's a Perfect Day by Abigail Pizer

The Pig in the Pond by Marta Waddell

Little Penguin's Tale by Audrey Wood

Letter Q

The Quiet Noisy Book by Margaret Wise Brown

The Very Quiet Cricket by Eric Carle

Letter R

The Runaway Bunny by Margaret Wise Brown

The Rainbow Fish by Marcus Pfister

Letter S

Seven Sillies by Joyce Dunbar

Swimmy by Leo Lionni

Sylvester and the Magic Pebble by William Steig

Silly Sally by Audrey Wood

Letter T

Two Tiny Mice by Alan Baker

The Teeny Tiny Woman by Paul Galdone

Tacky the Penguin by Helen Lester

My Teacher Sleeps in School by Leslie Weiss

Letter V

Very Last First Time by Jan Andrews

The Very Hungry Caterpillar by Eric Carle

The Very Busy Spider by Eric Carle

Letter W

The Wind Blew by Pat Hutchins

Willy Bear by Mildred Kantrowitz

Where the Wild Things Are by Maurice Sendak

Letter X

Hattie and the Fox by Mem Fox

Ox-Cart Man by Donald Hall

Letter Y

Yummy, Yummy by Judith Grey

Little Blue and Little Yellow by Leo Lionni

Letter Z

Zomo the Rabbit by Gerald McDermott

Zella, Zack, and Zodiac by Bill Peet

Ch Digraph

Chicka Chicka Boom Boom by Bill Martin Jr. and John Archambault.

A Chair for My Mother by Vera Williams

Sh Digraph

Sheep in a Ship by Nancy Shaw

Sheep in a Shop by Nancy Shaw

Th Digraph

Three Cool Kids by Rebecca Emberley

Juba This and Juba That by Virginia Tashjian

Wh Digraph

Why the Sky Is Far Away by Mary-Joan Gerson

What About Ladybugs? by Celia Godkin

Phonic Skills in Children's Literature

The books in the previous list are primarily for reading to students. However, most teachers want to know the types of books students should read as part of their early reading experiences. *Becoming a Nation of Readers* makes this statement:

> The important point is that a high proportion of the words in the earliest selections children read should conform to the phonics they have already been taught. Otherwise they will not have enough opportunity to practice, extend, and refine their knowledge of letter-sound relationships (Anderson et al. 1985, 47).

We also strongly suggest that these books primarily contain words in students' speaking vocabularies. When this is the case, students can often validate for themselves when they are using phonics correctly.

Finally, we return to *Becoming a Nation of Readers'* important admonition about the teaching of phonics: "Do it early. Keep it simple" (Anderson et al. 1985, 43). Teaching phonic skills long after they are necessary can be detrimental to students' ability to gain other, possibly more important, reading strategies. Taylor et al. (2003) report on their research completed in high-poverty schools across the United States. They examined the elements of classroom instructional practice that accounted for the greatest growth in student reading achievement. They found the following information:

- The occurrence of phonic instruction was greater in first grade than in grades two through five and the more that explicit phonic skill instruction was observed in grades two through five, the lower the growth in reading achievement.

- Across all grades, little higher-level questioning or writing related to texts was observed. Lower-level questioning was observed at higher rates.

- Across all grade levels, students were more often engaged in passive responding than active responding.

- Results indicated that teachers who emphasized higher-order thinking promoted greater student achievement in reading.

- Even limited levels of higher-level activities resulted in substantial growth in student achievement.

Their study suggests the essential focus of reading instruction must be to actively engage students in higher-level activities so that reading is seen as thinking from the beginning.

In short, as important as phonic skills are to reading success, they are only one component of the reading process. If over-taught, especially to the detriment of instruction related to higher-order thinking, students' reading achievement may be curtailed.

Concluding Remarks

Teaching phonic skills to students in the early grades is a viable instructional process; however, it certainly is not a perfect process. The sound-symbol relationship in the English language simply is not very regular. Fortunately, it does not have to be. Groff (1986) found that beginning readers can achieve reasonable approximations of words through the use of phonic skills. Generally, these approximations are close enough to words in students' speaking vocabularies to allow them to infer a successful pronunciation. Phonics can be especially productive when used in conjunction with structural analysis, the focus of the next chapter.

Important Points to Remember

- Phonics is an essential component of the word analysis process.

- Sound/symbol relationships vary from region to region and dialect to dialect.

- Words that students are asked to sound out should be in their speaking vocabularies.

- A little phonics can go a long way.

- Teach phonics early and keep it simple.

- The heart of the reading process is comprehension.

Post-Reading Reflection

1. Which phonic rules or generalizations do you think are essential to teach?

2. When do you think invented spelling should be curtailed?

3. How important is it that the sounds students associate with letters of the alphabet be similar to yours?

4. When should higher-order thinking be an important component of reading instruction?

Chapter 6

Structural Analysis

Structural analysis is often a neglected component of word analysis instruction. And, if it is introduced, it is generally in the third grade or later. We strongly suggest that structural analysis be a significant component of instruction and that it be introduced as an initial part of the word analysis process. One reason for this centers around our broad and simple definition of structural analysis. We define it as the process students use to analyze the structure of a word. When students look at the components of a compound word, become aware of affixes, or look for familiar "chunks" in words, we feel they are using the process of structural analysis. The process of structural analysis is an important tool for students when they begin to encounter multisyllabic words. Phonics can work reasonably well with one-syllable words, but it quickly becomes unwieldy with longer words. Just for fun, let us examine a word unfamiliar to many adults. The word is *pusillanimous*. Obviously, this word cannot be decoded by sounding out each letter in order. What seems most effective is to compare *pusillanimous* with words, or parts of words (chunks), that are known. The *pu* begins like *pupil*, *sill* rhymes with *bill*, and *animous* is familiar as in *unanimous*. While this is not a perfect process—*father* can quickly become *fat her*, for example—it is more viable than trying to teach students a set of rules for dividing words into syllables. Adams concurs, stating, "We can specify no fixed and final set of letter-based rules about how the mind will divide a word into syllables" (1990, 122).

We are firmly committed to the concept of compare/contrast or "chunking" and find much support for the process in literature (Adams 1990; Cunningham 2005; Gaskins, Gaskins, and Gaskins 1991; Gunning 1995; Manzo and Manzo 1995; Stahl 1992). We are also firmly committed to introducing this concept to students early, and we believe that one of the best ways to do so is through the process of onset and rime. Onset is the part of the word that comes before the vowel and rime is the rest of the word. Guiding students to become aware of rimes allows them to see that the relationship letters have to each other can strongly influence how they are pronounced. Becoming aware of rimes and larger word chunks frees many students from the more laborious sound/symbol process. Students are often thrilled to discover that once *at* is learned, adding a variety of consonant sounds that they already know allows them to read an amazing number of words. In this light, the 37 rimes introduced below allow students to derive nearly 500 primary-level words (Wylie and Durrell 1970).

ack	ap	est	ing	ore
ain	ash	ice	ink	uck
ake	at	ick	ip	ug
ale	ate	ide	ir	ump
all	aw	ight	ock	unk
ame	ay	ill	oke	
an	eat	in	op	
ank	ell	ine	or	

For older or more accomplished readers, an introduction to high-utility prefixes and suffixes is important. The following prefixes and suffixes have been identified as high utility (White, Sowell, and Yanagihara 1989). They and their percentage of usage for grades 3–9 are identified below.

Prefixes	
un-	(26%)
re-	(14%)
in-, im, ir-, il-	(11%)
dis-	(7%)
en-, em-	(4%)
non-	(4%)
in-, im-	(4%)
over-	(3%)
mis-	(3%)
sub-	(3%)
pre-	(3%)
inter-	(3%)
fore-	(3%)
de-	(2%)
trans-	(2%)

Suffixes	
-s, -es	(31%)
-ed	(20%)
-ing	(14%)
-ly	(7%)
-er,-or	(4%)
-ion, -tion, -ation, -ition	(4%)
-ible, -able	(2%)

Cunningham and Hall (1998) introduce what they call the "Nifty-Thrifty-Fifty." These 50 words contain many of the prefixes and suffixes presented above. By guiding students to learn the following 50 words, they gain the ability to transfer what Cunningham and Hall label "chunks" from these words to unknown words. Later in this chapter, we will discuss a chunking strategy developed by Cunningham, Moore, and Cunningham (1989) that introduces how to use the "transferable chunks" presented on the following page.

Nifty-Thrifty-Fifty and Transferable Chunks			
antifreeze	anti	international	inter, al
beautiful	ful	invasion	in, sion
classify	ify	irresponsible	ir, ible
communities	com, es	midnight	mid
community	com, y	misunderstanding	mis
composer	com, er	musician	ian
continuous	con, ous (drop *e*)	nonliving	non, ing
conversation	con, tion	overpower	over
deodorize	de, ize	performance	per, ance
different	ent	prehistoric	pre, ic
discovery	dis, y	prettier	er
dishonest	dis	rearrange	re
electricity	e, ity	replacement	re, ment
employee	em, ee	richest	est
encouragement	en, ment	semifinal	semi
expensive	ex, ive	signature	ture
forecast	fore	submarine	sub
forgotten	en	supermarkets	super, s
governor	or	swimming	ing
happiness	ness	transportation	trans, tion
hopeless	less	underweight	under
illegal	il	unfinished	un, ed
impossible	im, ible	unfriendly	un, ly
impression	im, sion	unpleasant	un, ant
independence	in, ence	valuable	able

Strategies for teaching students to use onset and rime, as well as the broader processes related to multisyllabic words, will now be discussed.

Strategies for Developing Structural Analysis Skills

1. Cunningham, Moore, and Cunningham present how the process of chunking or compare/contrast can assist students when they deal with more sophisticated multisyllabic words. They describe a lesson that guides students to see that a word like *entertainment* can be decoded by comparing chunks in it to chunks in words they already know.

   > This is a long word, but it is not a very hard word to figure out if you use some of the other words you know. Cover all but *enter*. The first chunk is a word you know. The second chunk you know from words like *maintain* and *contain*. On the board, underline the *tain*. Finally, you know the last chunk if you know *argument* or *moment*. Write *argument* and *moment* on the board, underlining the *ment* (1989, 70).

   The authors go on to say that we must remind students that if they use the probable sound of letters and the sense of what they are reading, they can figure out many more words than if they just pay attention to one of the items— letter sounds or what makes sense.

2. Select a student who has a familiar rime in his or her name. Pat might be a good choice. Using manila folders cut in half, write the letter *P* on one section and *at* on the other. Have Pat stand at the front of the room with both sections together spelling Pat. Then ask Henry to come to the front of the room. Give him one half of a manila folder with the letter *h* printed

on it. Ask him to say the sound the *h* represents. Then take the *at* from Pat and give it to Henry. Have Henry place his *h* with Pat's *at*, and then have him read the word. Do this with the first letter of other student names, as appropriate.

3. As a variation of the previous idea, have students stand at the front of the room with the letters *p*, *d*, and *b* held in front of them. Write *ig* on the board. Ask the class which student's letter will turn *ig* into an animal that is pink and has a curly tail. Have the student hold the appropriate letter in front of *ig* so that *pig* is spelled. Next, ask the class which student's letter will make a word that means *large*. Have the selected student stand in front of *ig*, and have the class say the word. Follow the same process by asking the class which student's letter makes a word that means "something you use a shovel for." Finally, write the sentence, *The pig can dig a big hole*, and ask for volunteers to read it. If time permits, read *If You Give a Pig a Pancake* or *If You Give a Pig a Party* (Numeroff 2000, 2005).

4. Gunning (1995) discusses "word building," where students are introduced to a rime such as *at* and then asked to decode a word such as *pat*. Once they are comfortable with *pat*, the *p* is replaced with an *h* and so on. When students have the *at* rime under control, review the word *pat* and then replace the letter *t* with an *n* and ask students to read the new word.

5. Using a process we call "Looking for Old Friends," introduce the book *Once There Was a Bull...(Frog)*, (Walton 1995). After reading the book to students, discuss the compound words found in the story. Guide students to understand why a grasshopper is called a grasshopper, a toothbrush a toothbrush, and the students' very favorite—why homework is called homework! Talk about the fact that sometimes bigger words contain "old friends"—smaller words they already know.

6. For more proficient readers, a variation of the previous activity can involve prefixes, root words, and suffixes. Write the word

unfriendly on the board. See if students can locate an old friend in the word. Hopefully they will find that the word *friend* is truly an old friend. Then discuss the prefix *un-* and the suffix *-ly* and explain that these are also old friends because students can already read the words *unhappy* and *gladly*.

7. Finally, haiku is an enjoyable way to reinforce the concept of syllables. The website Kidzone presents a haiku to help students remember the number of syllables in a haiku format:

> I am first with five,
> Then seven in the middle
> Five again to end.

Kidzone states that one of the more popular forms of haiku is called "What am I?" Students write a poem such as the following:

> Green and speckled legs,
> Hop on logs and lily pads
> Splash in cool water.

The poem can either then be read aloud or placed on a bulletin board, and the class is given the opportunity to guess the subject of the haiku.

Children's Books That Feature Rimes

The following books are by Dr. Seuss. They all offer an enjoyable way to encounter rimes. As in all of our literature selections, these books should be read to students to help them become familiar with the concepts being taught. After reading these books, teachers should not be surprised to see students choosing them to read independently.

- *The Cat in the Hat* (1987)

- *Fox in Socks* (1965)

- *Green Eggs and Ham* (1988)

- *Hop on Pop* (1963)

Concluding Remarks

Structural analysis is a robust companion to phonics. It supplies students with a tool, when used in tandem with phonics, that allows readers to decode longer single-syllable and multisyllabic words. Unfortunately, not all words can be sounded out, not even using the combined tools of phonics and structural analysis. This leads to sight words, the topic of the next chapter.

Important Points to Remember

- Phonics works reasonably well with one-syllable words, but quickly becomes unwieldy with longer words.

- There seems to be no consistently effective tool for dividing unknown printed words into syllables.

- Structural analysis is a necessary tool used in analyzing words and should be introduced earlier than third grade.

- Teaching students to compare and contrast chunks of unknown words with familiar chunks of known words is an effective word analysis strategy.

Post-Reading Reflection

1. Which structural analysis skills do you plan to use with your students?

2. How will you introduce the concept of "chunking" to students?

Chapter 7

Sight Words

In this chapter, sight words are defined, their importance presented, and strategies for teaching them introduced. Sight words are words that are recognized immediately without need of analysis. They are important for at least four reasons.

1. When students recognize words immediately, they find it easier to read fluently and to focus on the meaning of what they are reading. Analyzing unfamiliar words takes time, equanimity, fortitude, and often tenacity. Note: If you found yourself dealing with the word *equanimity*, how to pronounce it, and what it means, you may have also found yourself losing sight of the meaning of the sentence. Your reading was most likely less fluent and your comprehension less automatic.

2. Many of the highest-utility words in the English language cannot be sounded out. They are irregularly spelled words and need to be recognized by sight.

3. A rich sight vocabulary provides a good foundation for using strategies, such as compare/contrast and chunking. Once students can read *cat*, they quickly recognize the similarity to *fat*, *sat*, and *mat*.

4. A rich sight vocabulary gives students a good foundation for using phonics. For example, once students recognize the words *dime, kite, cake,* and *ride,* they begin to recognize a pattern that helps them identify long vowel sounds in other words as well.

It is important to remember that the focus of reading is comprehension. Teaching sight words is an important task as long as students understand the meaning or use of the words they are learning. Because of this fact, teachers must give attention to both structure words and function words.

Structure Words

Structure words are those words that have little meaning of their own. Their purpose is to maintain the structure of the sentence. Words such as *was, is,* and *the* are classic examples. Students find these words at best unexciting and, at worst, difficult to learn. Structure words should be presented in isolation as little as possible. These words make the most sense in context where they help hold function words together.

Function Words

Function words have importance in students' eyes. They usually have meaning even when encountered out of context. Words such as *teacher, student, dinosaur,* and *paycheck* are all function words with rich meaning. Examples such as the more derogatory four-letter forms of expression (We are talking about words that are, hopefully, seldom heard in the classroom!) are rarely forgotten by students, even when encountered only once. On a more positive note, an individual's name is an even more valuable function word.

While function words do not normally need context to give them meaning, there are two types that must have context. Homonyms and homographs are function words that need context to give them appropriate meaning. Homonyms are words spelled and pronounced the same way, but they have different meanings. Homographs are words spelled the same way, but they have different meanings and pronunciation.

The following two sentences show examples of homonyms. In these sentences, context supplies meaning.

> Please *hand* me the text with the definition of a diphthong in it.

> I now hold in my *hand* the text that defines diphthong.

The following sentences show examples of homographs. It is easy to see how context supplies both meaning and pronunciation.

> Let me *read* the text that defines diphthong.

> I *read* the text that defines diphthong.

Homophones, another form of function words, are words that are pronounced the same way, but are usually spelled differently and have different meanings. The meanings of homophones become more obvious when placed in context.

> Let me tell you a *tale* about why a dog has a *tail*.

It is obvious that sight words are important. However, what are the important sight words? The next section supplies some answers.

Sight Words

There is a common group of words that are of high utility for readers and writers. If students can learn the 100 words that make up 50 percent of all written material, they will have a significant foundation for learning the decoding process.

Appendix B has a compilation of high-frequency word lists. It was developed by comparing the lists of Carroll, Davies, and Richman (1971), Fry (1980), and Eeds (1985). The words chosen are those that can be located on at least two of the three lists. They are presented in approximate order of use. To be selected for the 50 words of highest frequency, the word must have appeared on all three lists. If students can learn the first 10 words, they will know approximately 25 percent of the words they will encounter when reading. If students learn all 100 words, they will know approximately 50 percent of the words they will encounter when reading.

High-Frequency Words in Literature

Eeds (1985) provides a list of books that contain a high percentage of her "bookwords." A portion of the list is provided. The list begins with books that have the fewest number of total words. The list also includes the number of different words presented in the book. For example, *Where's Al?* has 34 words, but a total of only 18 different words. As students read these books, they encounter and practice high-utility words on a regular basis.

Children's Books That Feature High-Frequency Words

Title and Author	Total Words	Different Words
Where's Al? by Byron Barton	34	18
Snake In, Snake Out by Linda Bancheck	38	8
The Friend by John Burningham	51	34
The Blanket by John Burningham	66	33
The Dog by John Burningham	69	48
Leo the Late Bloomer by Robert Kraus	70	66
Whose Mouse Are You? by Robert Kraus	108	54
The Chick and the Duckling by Mirra Ginsberg	112	30
Blackboard Bear by Martha Alexander	128	62
The Knight and the Dragon by Tomie dePaola	129	65
Shawn Goes to School Petronella Breinburg	132	75
There's a Nightmare in My Closet by Mercer Mayer	142	76
Little Gorilla by Ruth Bornstein	173	80
Everett Anderson's Goodbye by Lucille Clifton	200	104
Noisy Nora by Rosemary Wells	206	101
Let's Be Enemies by Janice Udry	229	102
Pinkerton Behave by Steven Kellogg	233	116
Move Over, Twerp by Martha Alexander	245	107
Little Blue and Little Yellow by Leo Lionni	284	123
Mr. Gumpy's Outing by John Burningham	289	95
Grandfather and I by Helen Buckley	291	79
The Stupids Die by Harry Allard & James Marshall	296	140
I Wish I Was Sick Too by Fritz Brandenburg	327	107
The Surprise Party by Pat Hutchins	336	101
Goggles! by Ezra Jack Keats	336	139
Where the Wild Things Are by Maurice Sendak	350	129
Avocado Baby by John Burningham	373	160

Title and Author	Total Words	Different Words
The New Girl at School by Judy Delton	379	158
Whistle for Willie by Ezra Jack Keats	391	149
The Stupids Step Out by Harry Allard	413	176
The Runaway Bunny by Margaret Wise Brown	441	83
Sand Cake by Frank Asch	443	153
Will I Have a Friend? by Miriam Cohen	464	277
The Stone Doll of Sister Brute by Russell & Lillian Hoban	494	143
Mine Will, Said John by Helen Griffith	506	124
Ask Mr. Bear by Marjorie Flack	632	118
George and Martha by James Marshall	645	210

Word Walls

Word walls are powerful agents for assisting students in learning sight words and improving their word analysis skills. Since there are practically as many different forms of word walls as there are teachers, we suggest that a word wall consist of the following to effectively enhance the word analysis process.

1. The list of 100 high-frequency words are presented in Appendix B.

2. Add the target words that students select to represent the sound/symbol relationships. For example, if students selected *echo* as the target word for the short *e* sound, then *echo* should be added to the word wall. The target words should be printed in a color, perhaps green, to highlight that they are target words.

3. Add target words for the high-utility rimes to the word wall. Read *There's an Ant in Anthony* (Most 1992) before the first rime target word is added to the word wall. In this story,

Anthony finds rimes and smaller words in larger words. In each case, the smaller word or rime is printed in red. After reading the book, add target words for rimes to the word wall. Print the onset in black and the rime in red, as in the book *There's an Ant in Anthony.*

4. All of the above words should be permanent components of the word wall. Add and/or remove seasonal words, holiday words, and words related to a unit of study, as necessary.

To effectively enrich the word analysis process, the word wall should be interactive. As students read, write, and are challenged by reading or writing a word, their first recourse should be to look to the word wall. When students ask for assistance, first take them to the word wall and show them how the wall can provide help. Incidentally, for students struggling with the word analysis process, help them develop their own personal word analysis dictionaries that contain many of the recommended words previously mentioned.

Sight Word Instructional Strategies

1. Some drill is necessary in teaching sight words. However, whenever possible, this drill must be fun and in the form of a game. More importantly, sight words need to be placed in meaningful context. Having students use sight words in meaningful ways in their writing is an effective technique for teaching students to personalize sight words. Once students master specific sight words, add the words to each student's personal dictionary. They can use these words in their writing. This is a simple yet powerful technique for making sight words personally valuable for students.

2. In order to reinforce sight words, place selected sight words on the wall around the door that students use to exit the classroom. Use no more than 10 words at a time and begin with the words of highest utility. We suggest the cards

containing the words be in the shape of a key. On the first day of this process, students must read at least one word before they receive the imaginary "key" to go out the door. On the second day, they must read two words, etc. Each student can read the same word or words as read by the student immediately preceding him or her. In this way, students see and hear sight words on a repeated basis. We have found that the words should be placed in a different location around the door every two to three days so that students remember words by their appearance rather than by their location. In addition, place words around the pencil sharpener, athletic equipment, or another appropriate location. To use the sharpener or get a soccer ball, students must read x number of words. This same process is effective with older students when they need to learn specialized content words.

3. Have students become experts for a specific number of words. For example, if you have 25 students, make each student an expert for four words. Print these words on the inside and outside of a manila folder. Keep the folder in students' desks. Keep a master list with the students' names and the words for which they are the experts. Give the easier, highest-utility words to the students most challenged by the word analysis process. When a student asks for help with a word, consult the master list and send the student to the expert for that word. The expert opens his or her folder, and the student who needs help points to the word in question. The expert reads the word, and both students benefit from the process.

4. A wonderful way to show students how much progress they have made is to have each student bring in a shoebox or another appropriate container. As they learn a word, print it on an index card. Have students place the index cards in their containers. When students have free time, they can read the cards in their containers. At the end of the school year, students take home the containers with all their words. Through the summer, they can read these words to parents, relatives, and anyone who visits their homes.

5. As mentioned earlier, games are appropriate tools for practicing sight words. Concentration, bingo, baseball, and word checkers are all enjoyable ways to learn sight words. Students of all ages love playing games. Concentration is played by simply using a set of sight word cards. Two cards for each word must be included in the set. Students can work in pairs or small groups. The cards are placed facedown, and students take turns turning two cards over at a time, looking for a match. Students who make a match keep the pair and take another turn until they are unable to make a match. Students quickly learn that this is a memory game and employ strategies for remembering the location of each card, as well as the word written on it. For those who are not familiar with word checkers, the game is very similar to the traditional checkers game. Cover the black squares on a checkerboard with sight words. Play the game the same as regular checkers, except have students say the word that is placed on the square before a checker is moved to that space. When selecting words to use in the game format for beginning readers, Manzo and Manzo (1995) indicate one key point to remember. Avoid words that look alike, such as *what/when*, and *their/then*. Just as with the initial teaching of the alphabet, it is best to select words that have clear differences. Choose words from a theme of study. For example, make a bingo game for each season of the year. Play the game with the whole class or in small groups.

6. Finally, authentic writing experiences are essential to building students' knowledge of sight words. Earlier, we discussed the importance of allowing students to use invented spelling. However, once a word appears on a word wall, it becomes a "No Excuse" word—if it's on the word wall, there is no excuse for misspelling it. Every time students write a sight word, it becomes more and more their own. There are a variety of authentic writing experiences we especially like, such as having students write to a pen pal. The pen pal can be a student in the same grade in another classroom in the same

school, an older or younger student, or a student from another school, state, or country. Students can write thank you letters to people who have done something special for them or the class. Examples include the custodian, someone who spoke to the class, the school librarian, or a substitute teacher. Writing to an important individual is powerful—especially when he or she writes back. Writing to the president of the United States, a major sports figure, or a special author provides authentic writing experiences for students.

Concluding Remarks

A powerful sight vocabulary is an important resource for readers. Students should be able to recognize words effortlessly so that they may read fluently and focus on making meaning. Ultimately, we would like for all words to become sight words. It is important to note that it is often those words that students do not recognize by sight that contribute most significantly to the meaning of the text. We are talking about specialized content words, such as *diphthong*, *schwa*, and *phonemic awareness*, and *penicillin*, *infection*, and *antibiotic*. To deal comfortably with these words, students must use all of the word analysis skills presented so far, as well as context clues. Context clues will be the topic of the next chapter.

Important Points to Remember

- The focus of reading is comprehension, even when learning to read sight words. Students must understand the meaning and use of these words.

- Many of the highest-utility words in the English language cannot be sounded out. They are spelled irregularly and need to be recognized by sight.

- Sight word growth is an excellent way to, in a very concrete manner, show students that they are making great gains in their reading.

- Ultimately, it would be ideal if all words become sight words.

Post-Reading Reflection

1. How would you answer concerned parents who want to know why their child should learn high-utility sight words?

2. What are four effective ways students can learn and retain sight words?

Chapter 8

Context Clues

The English Language

Bryson tells us, "But perhaps the single notable characteristic of English—for better and worse—is its deceptive complexity. Nothing in English is quite what it seems. Take the simple word *what*. We use it every day—indeed, every few sentences. But imagine trying to explain to a foreigner what *what* means. It takes the *Oxford English Dictionary* five pages and almost 15,000 words to manage the task. As native speakers, we seldom stop to think just how complicated and illogical English is" (Bryson 1990, 19).

As speakers of English, how did we get so comfortable with an often illogical language? How have we learned to deal with words as mysterious as *what*? We have met *what* time after time in context. Through repeated exposures to *what* in rich and meaningful settings, which includes listening to predictable books full of predictable language, we know what *what* is about. There is little doubt that *what* cannot be sounded out. The vowel sound just does not work very well. However, when we encounter *what* repeatedly in familiar and enjoyable books and use it often in important writing, we begin to make *what* our own.

What Is Context?

Context is the tool that ties the word analysis process together. Producing students who ask themselves the question, "Does this make sense?" when reading may be the single most important thing teachers do. Context is the tool that allows students to answer this question. Graves and Watts-Taffe (2002) state that, when it comes to word-learning strategies, the most widely recommended and most-used strategy is context. This chapter defines context, offers further justification for teaching it, supplies strategies for teaching it, and presents a list of predictable books for enhancing students' understanding and use of context.

When students use context clues, they are using the print surrounding an unfamiliar word to give it meaning and to help them pronounce it. Adams discusses context as follows: "Readers work with context to select (and, when necessary, re-select) the most appropriate meaning of the phrase as a whole" (Adams 1990, 413). Our statement and that by Adams lend credence to the concept that context is the tool that allows students to answer the most important question about what they are reading: "Does this make sense?" Context prevents students from over-relying on phonics and structural analysis. It keeps students from producing sentences such as "I saw Jada riding a *house* through the meadow." However, as essential as context is, it cannot stand alone. It must be used in balance with other word analysis tools. Students who use context, phonics, structural analysis, and a powerful sight vocabulary to approach unfamiliar words greatly increase their ability to read these words and make them their own. Let us look at how context works with other skills to guide students to unlock words. A word to question is *father*. If students used phonics alone, they might produce /fa/-/ther/ with a short *a*, or /fay/-/ther/ with a long *a* sound. If they used just structural analysis, they might see a compound word and produce

/fat/-/her/. But it is when they read a sentence like, "I have hair the same color as my father's," and see *father* in context, and then the word and sentence make sense.

It must be stressed that the use of context moves well beyond the sentence level. When students have a firm understanding of the books they are reading, they have created a context and know every word that they encounter should fit within that context. Students are logical and understand that scary stories have scary words and descriptive tales have descriptive words. It is the students who cannot create context who produce sentences such as "I saw Jada riding a *house* in the meadow."

Not all students naturally use context. This can be especially true of students who rely too much on sight words or phonics as they decode and those who do not have personally valuable reasons for reading. Fortunately, students can be taught to use context. We suggest such instruction start even before they begin to read.

Strategies for Teaching Context Clues

This section presents strategies for producing students who use context successfully. Focus will be on the following three concepts:

- developing students who have a reason for reading

- producing students who monitor their reading and continually ask themselves the question, "Does this make sense?"

- establishing the first two concepts before students have had formal reading instruction

Developing Students Who Have a Reason to Read

Students need to view reading as a personally valuable

experience. When a student picks up *Miss Nelson Is Missing* (Allard 1977) and says, "I want to read this," the chances are significantly increased that he or she will naturally use context. When a student looks at the cover of *Where the Wild Things Are* (Sendak 1963) and states, "Wow, look at those monsters!" the chances are great that he or she has developed a rich story context. We suggest guiding students to develop reasons for reading by taking two or three minutes to look at the cover together, read the title, examine the illustrations, and ask questions about the story before a story is read. Initially, teachers should model the question-asking process, then guide students to develop their own questions.

Developing Students Who Ask Themselves, "Does This Make Sense?"

We have said it before, and it is the perfect time to say it again: Asking the question, "Does this make sense?" is an extremely important characteristic of an effective reader. It is not something most readers do consciously. However, when something does not make sense, most individuals quickly stop and carefully examine the troublesome word or sentence. When a student reads, "I saw Jada riding a *house* in the meadow," it is a perfect time to interrupt a student's reading and ask, "Does that sentence make sense?" There are several strategies for developing "sensemaking" students. One that we like is called the cloze technique.

What Is the Cloze Technique?

Cloze is a technique in which the reader supplies deleted words in a sentence or passage by using syntactic (grammatical) and semantic (meaning-bearing) clues. It guides students to focus on meaning cues rather than just graphic cues. It assists students in using context clues when they can verify the appropriateness of a tentatively decoded word.

Cloze Activities

There are a variety of cloze activities. Some of our favorite cloze activities include the following:

- Activities where highly predictable words are deleted

  "_____ is a process where students associate sounds with written symbols."

- Activities where every third, fourth, etc. (i.e., a number of your choice) word is deleted

  "Phonics is a process _____ students associate sounds with _____ symbols."

- Activities where words are deleted but the initial letter or letter combination is supplied

  "Phonics is a process wh _____ students associate sounds with wr _____ symbols.

- Activities where words are deleted but students are given a choice of words to select

  "Phonics is a process _____ students associate sounds with written symbols." (who, where, what)

- Activities where just selected nouns, adjectives, verbs, etc. are deleted

  "Phonics is a process where _____ associate sounds with written symbols."

Cloze is a technique that enhances students' use and understanding of context. However, students' use of context develops most easily when they are introduced to the concept early in their literacy development. Toward this goal, children should be read to from the moment they can sit in a parent's lap. The language of literature should run through their heads. The more they hear this language, the more they understand how it works. It is the rare student who does not read along with *Brown Bear, Brown Bear, What Do You See?* (Martin 2007) or chime in "even in Australia" when Judith Viorst's *Alexander and the Terrible, Horrible, Not Good, Very Bad Day* (1987) is read. It is equally important to read to older students, especially as they approach content material. Having teachers read expository text to students on a regular basis allows students to more easily use context as they approach challenging words.

Working With Young Children

We have developed a strategy that is particularly effective for developing context in young children. When reading to students, simply pause when a highly predictable word is encountered. We have actually seen students lean forward, mouthing the word they know is going to come. When reading *I Know an Old Lady Who Swallowed a Fly* (Rounds 1990), pause just before *die* in the phrase, "I guess she'll die" and watch what happens. This simple strategy naturally develops a knowledge of context in a child's mind. A category of books called predictable and pattern books are best to use to develop this strategy. Some of our favorites follow. Publishing information for these books can be found in the Children's Literature Cited section.

Predictable and Pattern Books

- *Just Like Daddy* by Frank Asch

- *The Very Hungry Caterpillar* by Eric Carle

- *Five Little Monkeys Jumping on the Bed* by Eileen Christelow

- *The Little Fish That Got Away* by Bernadine Cook

- *Are You My Mother?* by P. D. Eastman

- *Up to Ten and Down Again* by Lisa Campbell Ernst

- *Where's Spot?* by Eric Hill

- *A House Is a House for Me* by Mary Ann Hoberman

- *1 Hunter* by Pat Hutchins

- *Herman the Helper* by Robert Kraus

- *Whose Mouse Are You?* by Robert Kraus

- *Ten Bears in My Bed* by Stanley Mack

- *Brown Bear, Brown Bear, What Do You See?* by Bill Martin Jr.

- *Fire, Fire, Said Mrs. McGuire* by Bill Martin Jr.

- *If You Give a Mouse a Cookie* by Laura Joffe Numeroff

- *Chicken Soup with Rice* by Maurice Sendak

- *There Was an Old Lady Who Swallowed a Fly* by Simms Taback

- *Alexander and the Terrible, Horrible, No Good, Very Bad Day* by Judith Viorst

- *Have You Seen the Crocodile?* by Colin West

- *The Napping House* by Audrey Wood

Additional sources for predictable and pattern books, as well as instructional strategies, can be found in Rhodes (1981), Atwell (1985), Cerbus and Rice (1995), Opitz (1995), and Saccardi (1996).

Concluding Remarks

Context is the powerful bridge between the word analysis process and comprehension. It is the final piece in the word analysis puzzle. It is the central component of students' personal logic of the code, and it prompts them to ask the question, "Does what I'm reading make sense?"

Important Points to Remember

- Context is the tool that ties the word analysis process together. Context clues help students verify the appropriateness of tentatively decoded words.

- Context is the central component of students' personal logic of the code. It prompts students to decide whether what they read makes sense.

Post-Reading Reflection

1. What strategies would you use to guide students to generate questions as they choose books?

2. What strategies would you use to guide students to ask themselves the question, "Does this word make sense in this sentence?"

Chapter 9

Fluency

Fluency and Active, Strategic Reading

As has been stated throughout this text, the primary function of the word analysis process is to allow students to comprehend what they are reading. In Chapter One, we made the following statement, "...to be successful readers, students must develop their own understanding of how our language works and then be able to decode words so fluently and naturally that all attention is given to understanding what is being read" (pp. 14–15). A key phrase in this statement is that *students be able to decode words so fluently and naturally that all attention is given to understanding what is being read*. Fluent reading often allows students to spend their cognitive energy not on the word analysis but on comprehension. This chapter discusses fluency and fluency's more important partner: active and strategic reading. It also includes Samuels' (2003) explanation about Stages of Word Recognition Skills and the importance of fluency instruction. Finally, it addresses strategies for promoting fluency and strategic reading.

Stages in Word Recognition Skills

Samuels (2003) presents the following three stages of word recognition skills:

1. Nonaccurate stage: Students have difficulty identifying words in a beginning reading text. This occurs during the early period of formal reading instruction.

2. Accurate but not automatic stage: With appropriate instruction, which includes exposure to a wide variety of skills such as reading in context as well as instruction in phonics, the student acquires the ability to recognize some words as "sight words" and other words by sounding them out. When listening to students at this stage read orally, one notes that the rate of reading is slow and laborious. Often the student has to sound out the words one part at a time and uses little expression in his or her voice. If students are unfamiliar with the topic of the text, they have little understanding or recall of what was read orally. To understand the passage, students must reread it several times.

3. Accurate and automatic stage (fluent stage): Students at this stage can read orally with accuracy, speed, and normal expression, as if they were speaking rather than reading from text; they can decode and comprehend simultaneously.

To this point, we have primarily focused on stages one and two. Now we will focus on stage three, Samuels' fluent stage, as well as the more important concept of active, strategic reading.

Importance of Fluency Instruction

The National Reading Panel (2000, 1) defines fluency as the ability to read with speed, accuracy, and proper expression. According to Samuels' fluent (third) stage of word recognition, it is essential to emphasize that when reading fluently, students should analyze words and comprehend simultaneously. Unfortunately, some teachers, schools, and districts push students to read faster and measure fluency success simply based on the reading rate, while losing sight that fluency is important because it allows students to spend their cognitive energy on comprehension. In short, fluency for fluency's sake should not be an instructional goal. It is essential that students read at a rate that allows them to gather meaning. Therefore, sometimes they must slow down. They must be active, strategic readers with a purpose for reading clearly in mind, and they must read in a manner that allows them to gain the knowledge they are seeking. Active, strategic readers know when to slow down and when to increase their reading rate. Take a moment to look at Samuels' second stage of word recognition. He states that if students are unfamiliar with the topic being read, they will have little understanding or recall of what was read orally. If students wish to understand a passage dealing with unfamiliar concepts and vocabulary, they often must reread the passage several times. We suspect that in reading this text, perhaps when examining something as unexciting as the definition of a diphthong, there were times when you were not functioning at Samuels' third stage of word recognition. If you were reading fluently but not strategically, you may have raced right through the definition of a diphthong and failed to clearly understand either its definition or purpose. Full understanding might not have been possible without rereading and struggling with the definition of a diphthong. Quick, can you define a diphthong? Do you need to return to Chapter Five and chase down the definition? In short, there is little doubt that without accuracy and fluency when decoding, comprehension can suffer and that improving reading fluency must be an instructional goal (Blachman 2000). However, it is essential that students know how to monitor their reading and slow down when accuracy and comprehension diminish.

Another important statement in Samuels' Stage Three is that "...students read orally with accuracy, speed, and normal expression, as if they were speaking rather than reading from text." Kuhn (2004) states that fluency involves reading with expression or prosody with students using pitch, stress, and appropriate phrasing. Prosody is important because when students read in a monotonous, word-by-word manner, comprehension often suffers.

In summary, fluent reading is the ability to read with accuracy, speed, proper expression, and appropriate phrasing while comprehending. Active, strategic reading is the ability to read with purpose and to interact with text while monitoring comprehension. Reading rate is adjusted accordingly, and rereading is used as needed. The remainder of this chapter focuses on instructional strategies for fluency and active, strategic reading.

Strategies for Teaching Fluency and Strategic Reading

The Poetry Academy

The Poetry Academy was developed by Wilfong (2008) based on a program called Fast Start (Padak and Rasinski 2008). Wilfong presents the following guidelines to promote fluency:

1. Give community volunteers a two-hour training session on the basics of repeated reading, listening-while-reading, modeling, and assisted reading.

2. Give each student a folder to keep copies of all the poems they read.

3. Have volunteers meet once a week for 5–10 minutes with a dysfluent student to read a short poem that is selected by the teacher, based on the student's reading level.

4. Have the volunteer read the poem to the student (modeling).

5. The volunteer invites the student to read the poem with her or him simultaneously.

6. The volunteer invites the student to read the poem independently and provides both assistance and praise.

7. At the conclusion of the session, the volunteer discusses with the student what the poem means to the student and analyzes any unknown words.

8. The student takes the poem home and reads it to as many individuals as possible and gathers signatures from listeners to verify readings.

9. The following week, the student reads the poem one more time to the volunteer to demonstrate mastery. The volunteer introduces a new poem.

10. At the end of the academic year, the students, their parents, and volunteers are invited to a Poetry Café. Students have the opportunity to read their favorite poems while everyone enjoys pizza.

Wilfong (2008) reports that not only did the Poetry Academy promote fluency, but it also brought humor and pleasure to the reading process for struggling students.

Anticipation Guides

An anticipation guide is a pre-reading and post-reading strategy that consists of statements designed to challenge and, in some cases, support students' current beliefs about a topic. For example, "Worms are boring" might precede a story demonstrating precisely the opposite point of view. Before reading, students should indicate whether they agree or disagree with the statement. After reading the selection, students respond to the same statement and indicate whether they agree or disagree with their original belief and then defend their responses. Much of their defense must come from information obtained from the material read. Through this process, students read more actively and strategically as they want to see if they were correct or not. They have a personally important reason to read. After reading the selection, students are asked to orally read supporting information from the text. This provides students with authentic reasons to reread sections of the material and promotes fluency. The following outlines how to guide students through this process.

1. Identify any major concepts and supporting details in a text.

2. Identify students' experiences and beliefs that will be challenged and, in some cases, supported by the material.

3. Create statements that might reflect your students' pre-reading beliefs concerning a topic that may challenge or modify such beliefs. See the statements below taken from *Biggest, Strongest, Fastest* by Steve Jenkins (1997). Include some statements that are consistent with your students' experiential background and with the concepts presented in the material to be read. Three to five statements are usually adequate.

Agree	Disagree	
_____	_____	The whale is the world's largest living animal.
_____	_____	The whale is the world's longest animal.
_____	_____	The flea, for its size, is the world's best jumper.
_____	_____	The whale, for its size, is the world's strongest animal.

4. Model the first statement for the students. Indicate that you agree with the statement because you have read books about whales and have seen programs on television that indicate

that this is true. Make an "X" in the "Agree" column. Explain to students that they must be able to justify why they agreed or disagreed with each statement.

5. Discuss the second statement as a class. Ask students whether they can think of any animals that might be longer than a whale. Respond to students' statements in a positive and straightforward manner. For example, if a student says that he or she disagrees with the statement because a giraffe is longer, respond that you know a giraffe is taller than a whale, but that you are not sure if a giraffe is longer. Say, "We will have to read this story to find out."

6. Once students are comfortable with the process, place them in small groups to indicate whether they agree or disagree with each statement by making an "X" in the appropriate column.

7. After reading the selection, model how to reflect on the first statement with the class. Indicate you made an "X" in the "Agree" column. Tell the class that it looks like the book supported your ideas. Orally read the page to the class. Ask students whether this information supports your belief. Talk about the second statement as a class. Students will have discovered that there is a jellyfish that is longer than a whale. Have a volunteer tell where to find this information, and ask students to turn to this page. Have another volunteer read the information aloud while the rest of the class follows along. Have each small group discuss the remaining statements together and whether they continue to support their original beliefs. Explain that they should read the supporting information aloud to their groups.

8. Have volunteers from each group read their supporting information to the class. Reinforce as appropriate.

An anticipation guide process serves to enhance students' ability to activate prior knowledge as they begin the reading process and motivates them to approach the learning task in an active, strategic manner. In addition, an anticipation guide provides students with authentic reasons for rereading a passage. It is not unusual for students to read some information four or five times before they have completed the process.

The following strategies are effective in promoting fluency and active, strategic reading:

1. Model fluent reading through predictable and pattern books. Predictable and pattern books help students hear the natural flow of our written language. Look to the list provided in Chapter Eight for some of our favorites. It is not unusual for students to recite the more predictable passages along with you as you read, and you should encourage this.

2. Promote repeated oral reading. The National Reading Panel (2000) strongly supports the concept of repeated reading. In this process, students reread a passage numerous times until they have achieved fluency with the passage. Generally, the passage is first read orally by an adult to students; then students read it silently. After reading the selection silently, students are asked to read it orally. They continue rereading the passage until they have achieved appropriate fluency. Teachers should evaluate both reading rate and prosody to ascertain whether students are achieving fluency. To be blunt, students often find repeated reading boring. Giving students the option to read to a parent, a relative, last year's teacher, the principal, a pet, or even a favorite stuffed animal, may make the repeated reading process more enjoyable.

3. Have students participate in choral reading activities. Choral reading is when students read together as a group. The selection chosen should be relatively short and not too

challenging for your dysfluent students. Always read the selection to students first before asking them to participate. Then read the selection a second time and have students read with you. Finally, have students read the material in choral fashion without you. Echo Reading and Call and Response are other ways to promote choral reading. Echo Reading is when you read the selection and then, in choral fashion, students read it back to you. With Call and Response, you read a short portion of a story, and then students read the next section, you read the next, and so on. This strategy is particularly effective with predictable and pattern books.

4. Engage in reader's theater productions. Through reader's theater, students perform a play, but rather than memorize their lines, they read them. The plays are based on dialogue-rich books. Students practice the play multiple times before they are asked to perform in front of a group. Through such practice, students read and reread passages numerous times and have authentic reasons for doing so.

5. Involve students in paired reading. Paired reading is a strategy where two students or a student and an adult alternate reading to each other. The process seems to work best when one student is a better reader than the other. However, there should not be a significant difference in the two reading levels because this may frustrate the less able reader.

6. Read informational text material to students. Reading expository material can be challenging, even for students who are very fluent with narrative material. Hearing how informational texts sound is an important first step in achieving fluency with such material.

7. Introduce text sets to students. Text sets, a collection of books related to a common topic or theme, can provide students with repeated exposure to common ideas, concepts, and vocabulary and enable fluency. Yopp, Yopp, and Bishop (2009) discuss

using text sets to create a learning unit in which students read extensively about an area of interest. For example, initiated by the first rainy day of the school year, the teacher can read Wood's (2004) *The Napping House*, a wonderfully illustrated, warm, and gentle book dealing with a lazy, rainy day. To make a rainy day a little more exciting, read Barrett's (1985) *Cloudy with a Chance of Meatballs*. With teacher guidance, students will want to learn more about rain. Make available and encourage students to independently read *It's Raining Cats and Dogs: All Kinds of Weather and Why We Have It* (Branley 1993), *Flash, Crash, Rumble, and Roll* (Branley 1999), and *The Cloud Book* (dePaola 1984). In each of these books, students repeatedly encounter words such as *precipitation, drizzle,* and *droplets*. In addition, encourage students to read weather-related poems such as "Rain" and "Lazy Jane" in Silverstein's (2004) *Where the Sidewalk Ends*. Through this rich reading process, fluency is enhanced as students encounter common concepts, language, and vocabulary.

8. Introduce students to popular authors. Most of us have favorite authors. We enjoy their subject matter and writing style. Once we have read one of an author's books, we read subsequent books in a fluent and engaged manner. The same can be true for students. The more books they read by an author they view as informative and enjoyable, the more fluent and active their reading becomes. For students in the first and second grades, some enjoyable authors are Arnold Lobel and his *Frog and Toad* books, Ludwig Bemelmans' *Madeline* books, the Jan and Stan Berenstain series, Laura Numeroff's *If You Give a Mouse...* books, and Marc Brown's *Arthur* books. Second and third graders find Howes' *Bunnicula*, Cleary's *Ramona*, Sobol's *Encyclopedia Brown*, Blume's *Fudge*, and Danzinger's *Amber Brown* books all appealing and consistent in their writing style.

9. Motivate dysfluent students to read on their own and provide them with easy-to-read books at their independent reading levels. It is rare that an individual would practice new

swimming strokes in cold, deep, and rough water. Practice initially takes place in warm, shallow, and safe water. Fluency for the dysfluent occurs in the same manner. Providing students with literature that is easy and interesting to read encourages practice, and practice is an important step toward fluency.

10. Invite guest readers into your classroom. These can be parents, older students, the school principal, and important members of the community. We have found that firefighters and police officers, in full uniform, are especially well received by students in the early elementary grades. They are great models of fluent reading.

Concluding Remarks

Schwanenflugel et al. (2006) state that it is critical to remember that fluency is an important bridge to comprehension but not an ultimate destination. The authors focus on the central idea of this chapter. Fluency for fluency's sake is not the issue. Fluency as a bridge from analyzing words to comprehension is the ultimate destination.

Important Points to Remember

- Fluent reading is the ability to read with accuracy, speed, proper expression, and appropriate phrasing while comprehending.

- Active, strategic reading is the ability to read with purpose and interact with the text while monitoring comprehension.

- Pushing students to read faster and measuring fluency success simply based on reading rate loses sight of the fact that fluency is important because it allows students to spend their cognitive energy on comprehension.

Post-Reading Reflection

1. How important is reading rate to increasing students' comprehension?

2. How would you guide students to understand the concept of active, strategic reading?

Chapter 10

Key Text Issues and the English Language Learner

This chapter will review 10 significant text issues, discuss each issue's relationship to English language learners (ELLs), and offer word analysis strategies for teaching ELLs. It is essential to remember that good teaching meets the needs of all learners, but ELLs often require instructional accommodations. Before beginning this review, it is important to make the following statement:

> *Word analysis is not a significant issue when discussing the English language learner.*

Now that we have your attention, it's important to explain this statement. We agree with Shannahan when he states, "It is not that English learners don't need to learn to decode, just that they tend to learn decoding pretty easily and their failures are more likely going on due to low English proficiency." (Shannahan 2008, 8). Shannahan goes on to state that given the findings of the National Literacy Panel for Language Minority Children and Youth (August and Shanahan 2006), providing instructional time for English learners to explicitly improve their oral English is a more successful path to reading success than placing them in intervention groups that focus on teaching basic reading skills. In short, word analysis skills are important for English language learners, but are often not their most critical need. Having said that, we cannot forget the importance of language growth for English learners as we return the focus to word analysis. The following information represents what we feel are 10 essential issues addressed in this text. Key concepts of each issue are discussed, followed by their importance to the English language learner. Finally, the chapter includes appropriate accommodations and instructional strategies for ELLs.

Ten Key Issues

Issue One:

Reading is an active and personal process of constructing knowledge from printed language. Though brief as this definition is, it has three important components, especially as they relate to ELLs. They are: (1) Reading is a process of constructing meaning. All students must recognize that the purpose of reading is to gain knowledge. This is the heart of the reading process. To help make this a reality for ELLs, attention must focus on the second component of our definition of reading. (2) Reading is an active and personal process. One of the key concepts teachers must instill in all readers is that they must have reasons to read and that these reasons should be personally valuable and important. This is especially true for those students whose cultural background is distinctly different from the author of the text they are reading. When they are assigned a reading far outside their experiences and areas of interest, students often see little reason for actively reading the selection. However, when students have a personally valuable reason for reading, they often read more actively and with greater understanding. They have important questions that they want answered and will actively read to find answers to their questions. Regardless of the literacy experience, it is essential that teachers guide ELLs to see reasons for participating in the reading activity. "Please read this story about steam shovels" or "It's time to read Chapter Two and answer the questions at the end" are often not sufficient motivation to encourage active reading. (3) Reading involves printed language. The concept that ELLs are communicating with an author's printed language seems to have the most obvious impact on the ease with which they learn word analysis skills. The more a student's language is like that of the author, the greater the chance that active communication will take place. When English learners are asked to decode words unfamiliar to them, words containing unfamiliar sounds, and words found within sentences with unfamiliar syntax, they find the word analysis process especially challenging.

Issue Two:

Students need to develop their own logic of how the word analysis process works and have the desire and confidence to use the process whenever it is needed. A quick review: Readers must have a variety of tools to lift the author's printed language off the page. Decoding supplies students with such tools. When students bring context clues, phonics, and structural analysis skills, as well as a rich knowledge of sight words to the page, they have the resources to change printed language into thoughts and ideas with which they can communicate. Ultimately, we want to produce readers who use word analysis skills so naturally and fluently that all of their attention can focus on gathering meaning from what they are reading. For this to happen, students need to understand the process so well that they develop their own logic of the code. No two students approach an unknown word in exactly the same way. They take the tools that they have been taught and use the ones that make the most sense and work best for them as they personalize the process. It is our task to ensure that students have been taught all essential word analysis options so that the personal logic of the code process they develop is as rich as possible. This is especially important for ELL students. The word analysis process with its 40-plus sounds represented by 26 letters of the alphabet can make phonics daunting for any student. It is essential that ELL students do not rely on phonics alone. They need to understand the concept of onset and rime, learn a rich core of sight words, and use context to verify that they are decoding successfully.

Issue Three:

Two of the most powerful predictors of reading success are letter-name knowledge and phonemic knowledge. The National Reading Panel (2000) states that letter-name knowledge and phonemic awareness are the two best predictors of reading success in both the first and second grades. One of the reasons they are such excellent predictors of reading success is their importance to phonics. When analyzing words, young students use phonics, associating sounds (phonemes) with symbols (graphemes) as a primary decoding tool. The use of phonic skills takes place most successfully when students are sensitive to the alphabetic principle: they are comfortable with the concept that words are composed of letters that represent sounds.

It is no surprise that Chiappe and Siegel (2006) state that phonemic awareness and letter knowledge are important factors that influence the learning of reading skills for English language learners. Yopp and Stapleton agree and indicate that developing phonemic awareness and knowledge of the alphabet with ELLs is easiest when they are phonemically aware and when they are comfortable with the alphabet in their first language. Current research indicates that a growing body of work with children from a range of ages suggests the phonemic awareness transfers from one language to another. It is stated, "The data indicate that phonemic awareness in the native language is not only related to phonemic awareness in the second language, but also to reading acquisition." (Yopp and Stapleton 2008, 376). It is essential that ELLs clearly understand the concept of the alphabetic principle so that they are aware that sounds are associated with the letters of the alphabet. They can more easily be led to see the importance of phonic skills when they have this understanding. An excellent process for assessing this understanding is to analyze students' creative spelling. When students' spelling reflects a reasonable sound-symbol relationship, (remembering that dialect and ending sounds will cause some typical inconsistencies and are not areas of significant concern), then you know that students are aware of the concept that words are composed of letters that represent sounds. The chances are strong that they are ready for instruction in the use of phonic skills.

Issue Four:

Word analysis must always be seen as a tool to comprehending what is being read and constructing new knowledge. A quick review: Without thinking, active communication cannot take place. Active communication is the process in which readers seek meaning. When the meaning being sought is personally valuable, the reading process is more active for the reader. In short, readers have questions that they want answered. In fact, one of the significant differences between good readers and poor readers is that good readers have a personal stake in their reading. They are involved in the process because they want to be. They read because they want to be entertained or have questions that they want answered. If there is one statement that summarizes good readers, it is this—good readers ask questions. One of the most important results of the reading process is that readers leave the printed page with more knowledge than they bring to it. For this to happen, students must bring experiences, concepts, language, and motivation to the reading task and use each of these to test what they are reading against what they already know and would like to learn. For the English learner, the process, without careful instruction, can be extremely challenging or even impossible. The English learner often brings experiences, concepts, and language significantly different from those of the author of the material that they are reading. Take a moment to read the following excerpt on a cricket match.

*It was a testing time and Zimbabwe will no doubt
rue missing the chance Leonard have to Bekker
when he was on 15 as the batsman chipped Streak*

through the square-peg. However, Percival is a nuggety battler who, inspired by Leonard, hung on grimly until some semblance of tempo began to return to his uncomplicated footwork and crisp timing. It was not pretty and the left-hander was reprieved when Strange dropped a very difficult chance at cover point as he cut at Streak. Curiously, the chance had more effect on Day, who disappeared behind the sandbags until just before lunch when he fell to Strange, his edged dab unluckily ricocheting off the wicketkeeper's pads straight to Alistair at first slip. Meanwhile, Leonard was beginning to take command. With the new ball taken and coming nicely on to the bat, Leonard's hundred came after he twice blazed Longa off the back foot for successive offside fours. It was a fine inning made under trying circumstances, and Leonard's animated celebrations showed that he was delighted with this one as he was with the brace he scored in Barbados three winters ago.

Were you able to read every word? Since the excerpt is written in English, you most likely decoded each word successfully. What was your level of understanding? We suspect, for the vast majority of readers from the United States, it is not very high. Cricket is not often played nor watched in the United States. Consequently, your knowledge of cricket may be limited, and your familiarity with concepts about cricket may be close to nonexistent. The language used—despite being English—is still likely unfamiliar. Now, imagine this excerpt printed in another language. It's probable that you would learn little about cricket. Before asking ELLs to read material that is far removed from their experiences, and in a new language, it is critical to take steps to enrich their experiences and draw connections between what they know and what they are being asked to learn. Preteaching is an essential instructional accommodation for ELLs.

Issue Five:

Phonics does not work very well, but it is an essential word analysis tool. A quick review: Phonics is the association of sounds with symbols. The printed word *cat* is made up of three symbols— the letters of the alphabet *c, a,* and *t.* Students using phonics attach the sounds /k/, /a/, and /t/ to these symbols. Because our alphabet consists of consonants and vowels, phonics is the process of giving sounds to single consonants, consonant clusters, single vowels, and vowel clusters. Why does phonics not work as well as we would like? We discussed this extensively in Chapter Five. However, there are some special concerns for ELLs. No other written language we can think of has words that end in blends. The *nd* in *blend* is an appropriate example. Because of this fact, ELLs tend to not pronounce the final consonant sound in words ending in blends. Also problematic is that most other languages use the letter *i* to represent long *e.* Consonant digraphs also can be challenging, especially *ch. Charlotte, Chuck,* and *character* create special confusion, and then there are words like *cello* where the *ch* is pronounced but is represented only by the letter *c.* Diphthongs in words like *oil, toy, out,* and *cow* can be disconcerting since they rarely produce sounds associated with the vowels involved. It is important to remember that dialect is not a significant issue in phonic skill instruction. When working with ELLs, sound-symbol consistency is more important than students associating Standard English sounds to symbols. Various leaders of the United States, especially those from Texas, Georgia, and Massachusetts, have brought very distinct dialects to the oval office. It seems appropriate that students from Mexico, South Korea, and Bulgaria be allowed to comfortably bring their dialects to the classroom and to the word analysis process. Ultimately, of course, it is essential that students understand the words that they are decoding; this leads to their understanding of what they are reading.

Issue Six:

Structural analysis is an often neglected component of the word analysis process. A quick review: Structural analysis is the analysis of the structure of a word. While phonics is reasonably successful with single-syllable words, it begins to break down with multisyllabic words. Consequently, the task of structural analysis is to break large words into more manageable units. For example, when seeing the word *cowboy* for the first time, students will often notice the smaller units *cow* and *boy*. Morphemic analysis is often used in place of structural analysis. Trying to break printed words into manageable units when seeing them for the first time can be a challenge for ELL students. The written word *father* is an interesting example. Pronunciations such as /fat/-/her/, /fay/-/ther/, or /făth/-/er/ all seem reasonable, especially for students that do not have the word in their speaking vocabulary. Teaching ELLs word families and using cognates are especially important to success in learning structural analysis skills. For those unfamiliar with the term, *cognates* are words related in meaning and form to a word in another language because the words have the same historical source (Vogt and Echevarria 2008). "Communication" (English) and "comunicación" (Spanish) are cognates.

Issue Seven:

Sight words need to be placed in meaningful context whenever possible. A quick review: Sight words are words that are recognized immediately without need of analysis. Sight words are important for a variety of reasons, but the most significant reason is that a strong majority of the words that students frequently encounter cannot be sounded out. Words such as *was*, *said*, *the*, and *to* do not effectively lend themselves to the use of phonics. Such words need to be memorized. For the ELL student, vocabulary growth is essential, and Fry and Kress (2006) state that sight word growth is an early step to vocabulary growth. In addition, it is a very concrete way to show ELLs that they are progressing as readers. Have students write every sight word that they have learned on an index card and place it in a personalized shoe box. This does wonders for young readers' confidence. Watching the shoe box fill over the year speaks volumes about the learning that has taken place. Finally, word walls and personal dictionaries are valuable instructional tools for expanding ELL students' sight vocabularies.

Issue Eight:

The use of context can provide students with reinforcement that they are using word analysis skills successfully. A quick review: Context clues use the print surrounding an unfamiliar word to give it meaning and to help a reader pronounce it. When students are reading the sentence "The _____ is a lizard that changes color," they quite often will fill in *chameleon* because they know the word makes sense. This is a critical issue for English learners. Because the written language that they encounter can be significantly different from their dominant language, ELLs must be read to, especially from books with predictable patterns. ELLs must become comfortable with the language of literature. This is true for Issue Nine, as well.

Issue Nine:

Reading fluently is important but not as important as reading strategically. A quick review: Fluency is critical to successful reading but not sufficient. Blevins (2001) states that students who read fluently find it easier to expend their cognitive energy on making meaning rather than struggling with analyzing words. Fluency can be especially challenging for ELLs. They are asked to read in a language not their own, one that often has a different syntax and vocabulary and one that has challenging words to decode. Couple this with the fact that ELLs are often asked to read material close to or at their frustration level, and it is obvious why fluency can be difficult for them to achieve. ELL students must be given ample opportunity to read and write in nonthreatening environments. For example, we have found that round robin reading can be especially threatening to ELL students. We agree with Hasbrouck and Tindal's (1992) contention that round robin reading is one of the most harmful techniques for developing fluency. For all readers, it is important to remember that fluency is desirable as it enhances all students' ability to understand what they are reading. Reading fast is not the goal of fluency instruction—comprehension is the ultimate goal. There will be times when students must slow down and read in a decidedly nonfluent manner if they are to truly understand what they are reading. When material is especially challenging, students must read strategically and read slowly as they struggle to decode words. Rereading passages can contribute to a student's better understanding. Reading rapidly is simply inappropriate with very challenging material. It is important to remember that fluency changes, depending on what students are reading and their familiarity with words encountered. Even very skilled readers may read in a slow, labored manner when reading texts with unfamiliar words or about unfamiliar topics. For example, readers who are usually fluent may not be able to read material far outside their knowledge base. For many, a medical or technical journal can be slow and cumbersome reading. The same is certainly true of a six grade ELL student studying world history.

Issue Ten:

Rich, personally valuable literature should always be associated with the word analysis instructional process. Throughout this book, we have stressed the importance of using rich literature as a key component of the word analysis instructional process. Students are best motivated to use and practice their skills with material that is interesting or relates to something that they really want to learn. Good, rich literature can provide this for ELLs. After taking a field trip to the zoo and seeing an anaconda for the first time, it is rare that a student will not be motivated to read *The Day Jimmy's Boa Ate the Wash* (Noble 1992). In this story, Jimmy takes his pet anaconda on a field trip, much to the dismay of his teacher. Students bring prior knowledge—they now know something about anacondas and they want to find out more about really big snakes. Again, once ELLs see personal reasons for reading, they often find increased motivation to learn and use the skills of reading. To be blunt, there is nothing very motivating about learning blends or the silent *e* rule. However, when such knowledge will help students read the word *snake,* then motivation for learning word analysis skills is heightened.

English Language Learner Instructional Accommodations

This section of the chapter focuses on the instructional accommodations necessary for English language learners, followed by strategies that incorporate these accommodations. Much literature (Bear et al. 2006; Dunlap and Weisman 2006; Yopp and Stapleton 2008; Vogt and Echevarria 2008) suggests that the following instructional accommodations are important for successful word analysis learning for ELL students:

- The mystery must be taken out of instruction. ELLs need to know the purpose of the activity in which they are going to participate. Announce the lesson's objectives and activities, and list instructions step by step. Provide frequent summations of the salient points of a lesson and always emphasize key vocabulary words. Present new information in the context of known information.

- Develop and maintain routines. Use clear and consistent signals for classroom instructions. Instruction should be explicit and systematic.

- Preteaching activities are essential. What must students know to help them achieve success with the upcoming activity in which they will engage?

- Concepts must be presented verbally and in writing. ELLs need multiple ways to understand important skills and concepts. Enunciate clearly, but do not raise your voice. Add gestures, point directly to objects, or draw pictures when appropriate. Write clearly, legibly, and in print—many ELLs have difficulty reading cursive. Try to avoid idioms and slang words. Repeat information and review frequently. If a student does not understand, try rephrasing or paraphrasing in shorter sentences and simpler syntax. Check often for understanding, but do not ask "Do you understand?" Instead, have students demonstrate their learning to show comprehension.

- Provide feedback on correct and incorrect responses as soon as possible. All learners, but especially ELLs, need timely feedback about their success with learning important skills and concepts. Such feedback assists ELLs in their ability to internalize what works and does not work for them. Recognize student success overtly and frequently. But, also be aware that in some cultures overt, individual praise is considered inappropriate and can therefore be embarrassing or confusing to the student.

- Additional opportunities to practice are a necessity. As they are being asked to read and write in a second language, ELLs need at least 50 percent more practice time using essential skills than students learning to read in their native language. To provide time for practice, it is recommended that the instructional focus be on fewer but more essential literacy skills to allow additional time for ELLs to practice these skills.

Teaching Word Analysis Skills to English Language Learners

The following are important concepts and strategies to keep in mind when teaching word analysis skills to English language learners.

1. The words that ELLs are asked to decode must be in their speaking vocabularies. This allows students to know if they have used their word analysis skills successfully. In addition,

these words should be placed in context as soon as possible. In this way, students provide their own reinforcement as to what does and does not work for them. For example, when students are asked to decode the word *fire,* they encounter a word containing two competing "rules" they have been taught: the vowel+*r* and the silent *e* rule. When using the silent *e* rule, they will pronounce the word correctly and make the *i* long and the *e* silent. If they use the vowel+*r* rule, they may end up with /fur/-/ee/, with the *i* controlled (influenced) by the *r* and the *e* long. If *fire* is in their speaking vocabularies and is placed in context, "The fire burned down the house," ELLs begin to develop their own "logic of the code" and understand what and when word analysis skills work for them.

2. Word walls are essential instructional tools. These word walls should include a minimum of 100 sight words as well as student-selected target words for the sound-symbol relationships and word families taught.

3. Vowels can be challenging. When teaching vowels, hold the vowel sound so ELLs can clearly hear them. Do not hesitate to get ELLs involved as vowel sounds are reinforced. Have Edwina walk from one side of the classroom to the other. Have her say and extend the short *e* sound in her name as she walks across the room. Tell her not to pronounce her full name until she reaches the other side—Eeeeeeeeeeeeeeeeeedwina!

4. Students must internalize English spelling patterns. Target words representing high-utility rimes or word families are especially effective in this regard. Once ELLs have learned the word *at,* guide them to discover that it is an important component of such words as *cat, fat,* and *sat.* Have students vote on which word should be their target word for the rime *at,* and place that word on the word wall. Remember that the rime component of the target word should be printed in red ink. To further internalize the process, read students *The Cat in the Hat* (Seuss 1987).

5. No other written language that we can think of has words that end in blends. The *nd* in *blend* is a good example. It is common among ELLs when reading or spelling words ending in blends to eliminate the concluding sounds. One effective way to assist students in attending to such sounds is to pronounce all but the final consonant of a word ending in a blend and then ask students to provide the ending sound. This assists ELLs in focusing on ending blends. For example, take the word *and* from your word wall. Pronounce the word, then add *h* to *and* to make the word *hand*. Pronounce *hand*, then say all but the ending *d* (*han*). Guide students to pronounce the missing /d/ sound. Find other target words that end in blends and continue the process. Review on a consistent basis.

6. Teach the most common roots, prefixes, and suffixes (*re-, dis-, un-, cover, -pute, -ed, -able, -ly*). Learning these will allow students to possibly read thousands of words. If students are comfortable with the concept of rimes or word families, introduce them to high-utility common roots, prefixes, and suffixes. Teach students to look for old friends—roots and words that they already know. Have them examine the word *unfriendly*. Guide them to locate the word *friend* by removing both *un* and *ly*. Find target words with *un* and *ly*. Tell students that they are becoming good readers and should not to be afraid to try to read new words. Take the prefix *un* from *unfriendly* and add it to *afraid*, producing the word *unafraid*. Let students know that they should be unafraid of larger words when they know to look for old friends.

7. Students must be read to. They need to hear the language of literature—both narrative and expository. Do not hesitate to make slight pauses just before reading predictable words. You should not be surprised if students call out the word you are just about to read. For example, when reading *Alexander and the Terrible, Horrible, No Good, Very Bad Day* (Viorst 1987) make a slight pause just before the word *day* in the sentence, "It was a terrible, horrible, no good, very bad day." Pause just before *Australia* when reading the phrase "...even

in Australia" for the second and all subsequent times they are encountered in the book. This makes the listening process more active and guides ELLs to become more comfortable with the predictability of sentences.

8. Individual dictionaries are important writing and word analysis tools. In a sense, they can function like individual word walls for ELLs, containing sight words as well as student-selected target words for the sound-symbol relationships and word families taught. Individual dictionaries are especially effective for ELLs because students can add words of special interest to their personal dictionaries.

9. Writing reinforces the word analysis skills that ELLs have learned and makes such skills more concrete and real. Reading Noble's (1992) *The Day Jimmy's Boa Ate the Wash* and then writing a story about a really big snake reinforces both the *sn* blend and the silent *e* rule. Writing also enriches students' knowledge of syntax and how sentences work. For those ELLs just moving into the writing process, allow creative spelling and encourage it. When students come to recognize that the sounds in their language can be mapped onto alphabetic letters and they can use this knowledge in their writing, they have established a strong foundation for learning word analysis skills.

The following section discusses the Language Experience Approach and how it might be used to promote ELLs' learning of productive word analysis skills using several of the accommodations and strategies presented in this chapter.

Language Experience Approach

It rare to find a classroom that does not contain students from more than one culture. Rarer still are teachers that are comfortable with all of the languages spoken by their students. Therefore, a reasonable strategy to use is the Language

Experience Approach (LEA). This approach, formalized by Allen, stresses the following:

What I can think about, I can talk about.
What I can say, I can write (or someone can write for me).
What I can write, I can read.
I can read what others write for me to read.
(Allen 1968)

This approach helps young students understand that the words they encounter in books are really just "talk written down." What makes this approach potentially effective for teaching word analysis skills to ELLs is that the words students encounter are their very own words, words already in their speaking vocabularies.

The Language Experience Approach begins with a shared, important experience. Perhaps students go on a class field trip to the zoo. Upon returning, they can hardly wait to talk about their experience. The teacher asks students to tell about their experience. On chart paper, the teacher writes, word for word, what the students tell her. Some teachers are uncomfortable with this and make minor corrections as students dictate. Either method is fine as long as students see that the story unfolding is clearly their own. After writing each sentence, the teacher reads it back to the class. This confirms to the students that the story is, indeed, their story. It is appropriate for the teacher to guide the process. Asking questions such as, "What other animals did you see?" or "What was exciting about the monkeys?" can often enrich the story and its potential to help with the word analysis process. Once the story is complete, the teacher reads it back to the students and asks for a good story title. If students cannot come up with a title, the teacher can provide choices, such as "Our Trip to the Zoo" or "Room 7 Visits the Zoo." As students read their words about their experience aloud, they are building their reading vocabularies. From here the teacher can personalize the lesson to focus on language arts concepts in which the class needs instruction or practice. The following is a story that students might provide after a field trip to the zoo. The teacher has taken the liberty to make minor corrections and occasionally guide the process, but students still see the story as their own:

> **Our Trip to the Zoo**
>
> Today we went to the zoo. We went on a bus. It took a long time to get to the zoo. At the zoo we saw snakes, a peacock, and stinky pink flamingos. Julio called them "stinky pinkies." We saw bears. We saw tigers. We saw a sleeping lion. We saw a scary black leopard. We saw two elephants. We saw three giraffes. We saw two camels. We saw a crocodile. We saw a fat hippo and we saw the world's biggest snake.
>
> We took our own food. A bird flew out of a tree and took Rosario's sandwich. Rosario was mad. Ms. Joline gave Rosario some of her lunch. At lunch, a zoo lady told us about the zoo. She said zoos are important. They help the animals from being extinct. After lunch, we took the bus back to school.
>
> We want to go back to the zoo.

This story, reflecting student experiences, language, and interests can be used for a multitude of literacy activities from sequencing to comprehension questions. The following are three word analysis strategies that might be introduced.

1. Letter Sounds

    a. Review student names that start with the /b/ sound. As you say their names, extend the /b/ sound.

    b. Then find three words that begin with the letter *b* in the students' language experience story. Three obvious choices are *bear, bird,* and *bus.* Read the complete sentence in which each word appears, and then clearly pronounce the word and extend the /b/ sound.

c. Write all three words on the board and pronounce them again while underlining the letter *b*.

d. Have students whose names start with the letter *b*, perhaps, *Belinda* and *Bernardo*, write their names on the board, pronounce their names, and underline the letter *b* in their names.

e. Let the class know that they have reviewed the *b* by isolating the sound and pronouncing it as a group.

f. It would be ideal at this point to read the class a book such as Peet's (1984) *Big Bad Bruce* to show that the letter *b* is important to enjoyable literature.

2. Using Context Clues

Again, as stressed previously in Issue Eight, the use of context can provide students with reinforcement that they are using word analysis skills successfully. All students benefit from immediate reinforcement, but this is especially true of English learners. When English learners successfully use context as one important aspect of the word analysis process, they are providing their own immediate reinforcement. The following might be used with the students' zoo language experience story.

a. Read the complete zoo story to the class, pausing at predictable words. For example, when reading the sentence, "It took a long time to get to the zoo," pause just a moment before the word *zoo*. This often allows students to mentally complete the sentence and add the word *zoo* on their own.

b. Write the following sentence on the board: "After lunch, we took the _____ back to school." Read the sentence to students, and leave out the missing word. Tell the class that the missing word must make sense in the sentence. Give students three possible choices, perhaps *hippo*, *bus*, and *zoo*. Read the sentence with each word in place of the missing word. Tell the class that you think *zoo* doesn't fit because you could not take the whole zoo back to school. Ask for a volunteer to tell you which of the remaining words makes sense. Provide appropriate praise for the correct choice.

c. Write the following sentence on the board: "A _____ flew out of a tree and took Rosario's sandwich." Ask for a volunteer to provide the missing word. After the sentence has been successfully completed, guide a class discussion as to why *bird* makes sense in this sentence. Discuss such things as birds roost in trees and can fly. Again, praise as appropriate.

d. Review the fact that good readers ask themselves "Does this sentence make sense?"

e. For fun, do a Mad Lib with the class. There is a Mad Lib website where teachers can locate appropriate Mad Libs.

3. As mentioned earlier, English is one of only a few languages that has words ending in blends. Because of this, English learners need to receive additional instruction on blends. Use the zoo language experience story as follows to enhance an understanding of blends.

a. On the board, write the words *bird, leopard, snake,* and *elephant*. Show students where you found the words in their story. Read the words and then read the sentences in which they were found. Review with students that blends are two or more letters working together and that they can be found at the beginning of words, like the *bl* in *blend* or at the end of words like the *nd* in *blend*.

b. Read the word *bird* again, stressing and extending the /r/ sound and the /d/ sound in the *rd* blend. Read it again and ask students to say the word along with you as you stress and extend both the *r* and *d* sounds.

c. Read the word a third time but do not pronounce the ending *d* sound. Ask the class to provide the sound. Say /bir/ and extend and stress the /r/ and ask the class to provide the /d/.

d. When students are able to provide the final /d/ sound, repeat the process with the word *leopard* since it has the same ending blend.

e. When the class seems comfortable with the *rd* blend, repeat the same steps with the *sn* blend at the beginning of *snake*.

f. Review with students that blends are two or more letters that work together and that they can be found at the beginning of words, like the *bl* in *blend* or at the end of words, like the *nd* in *blend*. Explain that students worked on ending blends today.

4. Extend the lesson by reading Noble's (1992) *The Day Jimmy's Boa Ate the Wash*.

a. Before reading, have students examine the book's cover. Ask them to identify the animals on the cover. Discuss which animals they might find in the zoo. Lead students to see that the really big snake on the cover is like the snake they saw at the zoo. Guide students to understand that the snake is eating someone's wash and that this snake is probably Jimmy's boa. Let them know that *boa* is short for *boa constrictor*. Ask students if this is the type of snake they saw at the zoo.

b. Explain that this story is about a field trip to a farm like their field trip to the zoo. Ask if they think Jimmy took his boa on the field trip to the farm. Be supportive of all reasonable answers. Then read the story. After reading the story, draw correlations between the field trip in *The Day Jimmy's Boa Ate the Wash* and their field trip to the zoo. In this way, students can better understand the relationship between their own written story and stories such as *The Day Jimmy's Boa Ate the Wash*. Use a T-chart to compare the two stories.

Our Trip	Jimmy's Trip
• zoo	• farm
• bus	• bus
• class	• class
• snake	• boa constrictor
• stinky pinkies	• stinky pigs
• a bird took Rosario's sandwich	• the boa wound into the wife's laundry

The Language Experience Approach can be a powerful tool for teaching ELLs word analysis strategies. We agree with Peterson et al. (2000), who state that this approach allows students to bring their personal experiences and language into the classroom, and this is especially important for English learners.

Websites

The following websites are highly recommended for teachers who work with English language learners. We are aware that websites do come and go, but these three sites have been in existence for some time and provide excellent information and strategies.

http://www.cal.org/siop

The SIOP (Sheltered Instruction Observation Protocol) Model is a research-based and validated model of sheltered instruction.

Professional development in the SIOP Model helps teachers plan and deliver lessons that allow English learners to acquire academic knowledge as they develop English language proficiency.

http://www.readwritethink.org

ReadWriteThink, established in April of 2002, is a partnership between the International Reading Association (IRA), the National Council of Teachers of English (NCTE), and the Verizon Foundation. The purpose of ReadWriteThink is to provide educators and students with access to the highest quality practices and resources in reading and language arts instruction through free Internet-based content.

http://www.nwrel.org

Established in 1966, The Northwest Regional Educational Laboratory (NWREL) has been working to make a difference in students' lives and in the lives of those who support their learning. NWREL is a private nonprofit organization that works closely with schools, districts, and other agencies to develop creative and practical solutions to important educational challenges.

Concluding Remarks

This book began by stating our bias about the environment in which students best gain their own logic of the code and develop effective and efficient word analysis skills. It is a balanced environment where students are given authentic reasons to read and write and are systematically provided with instruction that allows them to do so. This type of environment creates momentum in the classroom—momentum is created when students see a reason for learning what is being taught. They see a reason for coming to school each day. Chall (1967) tells us that one of the best ways to stop momentum in a classroom is to have students do unmonitored seatwork, especially with workbooks and drill-type worksheets. *Becoming A Nation of Readers* (Anderson et al. 1985) tells us it is not unusual to have students doing 1,000 worksheets a year. Adams reports on a longitudinal study of children in a Texas school. In this study, it was found that 40 percent of the lower-income fourth graders claimed that they would rather clean their rooms than read. One child stated, "I'd rather clean the mold around the bathtub than read" (Adams 1990, 5). Strickland and Cullinan, as cited in Adams, state:

> If learning is to occur, we must give children good stories that intrigue and engage them; we must give them poetry that sings with the beauty of language; we must enchant them with language play; and we must give them opportunities to write. In short, we must surround them with literature that helps them understand their world and their ability to create meaning (428).

Strickland and Cullinan would be greatly encouraged by the contents of *Reading on the Rise* (NEA 2009). This report, prepared by the National Endowment of the Arts, documents that after more than a quarter-century of decline, there has been a decisive and unambiguous increase in literary reading among virtually every group measured. The report states, "Best of all, the most significant growth has been among young adults, the group that had shown the largest declines in earlier surveys. The youngest group (ages 18–24) has undergone a particularly inspiring transformation from a 20 percent decline in 2002 to a 21 percent increase in 2008—a startling level of change" (1). Based on this report, Dana Gioia, Chairman of the National Endowment of the Arts, congratulates "the legions of teachers, librarians, writers, parents, public officials, and philanthropists who helped achieve this renascence" (2).

On such a positive note, we conclude this text with a simple formula for the complex and important process of producing students who both can and do read:

great literature + great instruction + time to practice
= great readers

Important Points to Remember

- It is essential to remember that good teaching meets the needs of all learners, but English language learners often require instructional accommodations.

- The mystery must be taken out of instruction. ELLs need to know the purpose of the activity in which they are going to participate.

- Word analysis skills are important for ELLs but are often not the most critical need.

- The words ELLs are asked to decode must be in their speaking vocabularies. This allows students to ascertain whether they have used their word analysis skills successfully. In addition, these words should be placed in context as soon as possible. In this way, students provide their own reinforcement as to what does and does not work for them.

- ELLs must have additional opportunities to practice skills learned. ELLs, as they are being asked to read and write a second language, need at least 50 percent more practice time using essential skills then students learning to read in their native language. To provide time for practice, it is recommended that the instructional focus be on fewer but more essential literacy skills.

Post-Reading Reflection

1. What is your definition of reading?

2. What are the essential word analysis skills you would teach to your students?

3. How will you guide students to gain essential word analysis skills?

Appendix A

Yopp-Singer Test of Phoneme Segmentation

Student's name _____

Date _____

Score (number correct) _____

Directions: Today we're going to play a word game. I'm going to say a word and I want you to break the word apart. You are going to tell me each sound in the word in order. For example, if I say *old*, you should say "/o/-/l/-/d/." (Administrator: Be sure to say the sounds, not the letters, in the word.) Let's try a few together.

Practice items: *ride, go, man* (Assist the student in segmenting these items as necessary.)

Test items: *(Circle those items that the student correctly segments; incorrect responses may be recorded on the blank line following the item.)*

1. dog	7. grew	13. race	19. at
2. keep	8. that	14. zoo	20. top
3. fine	9. red	15. three	21. by
4. no	10. me	16. job	22. do
5. she	11. sat	17. in	
6. wave	12. lay	18. ice	

°The author, Hallie Kay Yopp, California State University, Fullerton, grants permission for this test to be reproduced. The author acknowledges the contribution of the late Harry Singer to the development of this test.

Appendix B

High-Frequency Word List

1. the	26. what	51. him	76. has
2. and	27. we	52. us	77. way
3. a	28. can	53. an	78. bike
4. to	29. this	54. or	79. make
5. in	30. not	55. no	80. did
6. you	31. she	56. my	81. could
7. of	32. your	57. which	82. more
8. it	33. when	58. would	83. two
9. is	34. had	59. each	84. day
10. he	35. as	60. how	85. will
11. that	36. will	61. do	86. come
12. was	37. on	62. go	87. get
13. for	38. up	63. about	88. down
14. I	39. out	64. could	89. now
15. his	40. there	65. time	90. little
16. they	41. do	66. look	91. than
17. with	42. from	67. them	92. too
18. are	43. were	68. many	93. first
19. be	44. so	69. see	94. been
20. but	45. her	70. like	95. who
21. at	46. by	71. these	96. people
22. one	47. if	72. me	97. its
23. said	48. their	73. words	98. water
24. all	49. some	74. into	99. long
25. have	50. then	75. use	100. find

References Cited

Adams, M. J. 1990. *Beginning to read: Thinking and learning about print.* Cambridge, MA: MIT Press.

Allen, R. V. 1968. How a language-experience program works. In *A decade of innovations: Approaches to beginning reading,* ed. E. C. Vilscek. Newark, DE: International Reading Association.

Anderson, R. C., E. H. Hiebert, J. A. Scott, and J. A. G. Wilkerson. 1985. *Becoming a nation of readers: The report of the Commission on Reading.* Washington DC: The National Institute of Education.

Atwell, M. A. 1985. Predictable books for adolescent readers. *Journal of Reading* 29 (1): 18–22.

August, D., and T. Shanahan. 2006. *Developing literacy in second language learners.* New York: Routledge.

Bailey, M. H. 1967. The utility of phonic generalizations in grades one through six. *The Reading Teacher* 20 (5): 413–18.

Balmuth, M. 1982. *The roots of phonics*. New York: Teachers College Press.

Bear, D., L. Helman, M. Invernizzi, and S. Templeton. 2006. *Words their way with English learners*. New York: Prentice Hall.

Bishop, A. L. 1978. My daughter learns to read. *The Reading Teacher* 32 (1): 4–6.

Blachman, B. A. 2000. Phonological awareness. In vol. 3 of *Handbook of Reading Research*, ed. M. L. Kamil, P. B. Mosenthal, P. D. Pearson, and R. Barr, 483–502. Mahwah, NJ: Lawarence Erlbaum Associates.

Blevins, W. 2001. *Building fluency: Lessons and strategies for reading success*. New York: Scholastic.

Bradley, B., and J. Jones. 2007. Sharing alphabet books in early childhood classrooms. *The Reading Teacher* 60 (5): 452–63.

Bryson, B. 1990. *The mother tongue: English and how it got that way*. New York: William Morrow and Company.

Burmeister, L. E. 1968. Usefulness of phonic generalizations. *The Reading Teacher* 21 (4): 349–56, 360.

Carroll, J. B., P. Davies, and B. Richman. 1971. *Word frequency book*. Boston: Houghton Mifflin.

Cerbus, D. P., and C. F. Rice. 1995. *Whole language units for predictable books*. Westminster, CA: Teacher Created Materials.

Chall, J. S. 1967. *Learning to read: The great debate*. New York: McGraw-Hill.

Chaney, J. H. 1993. Alphabet books: Resources for learning. *The Reading Teacher* 47 (2): 96–104.

Chiappe, P., and L. S. Siegel. 2006. A longitudinal study of reading development of Canadian children from diverse linguistic backgrounds. *The Elementary School Journal* 107 (2): 135–52.

Clymer, T. 1963. The utility of phonic generalizations in the primary grades. *The Reading Teacher* 16 (4): 252–58.

Cunningham, P. M. 2005. *Phonics they use: Words for reading and writing*. 4th ed. Boston: Pearson/Allyn & Bacon.

Cunningham, P. M. and D. P. Hall. 1998. *Month-by-month phonics for upper grades*. Greensboro, NC: Carson-Delosa.

Cunningham, P. M., S. Moore, and J. Cunningham. 1989. *Reading in the elementary classroom: Strategies and observations*. New York: Longman.

Dunlap, C. Z., and E. M. Weisman. 2006. *Helping English language learners succeed*. Huntington Beach, CA: Shell Education.

Eeds, M. 1985. Bookwords: Using a beginning word list of high frequency words from children's literature K–3. *The Reading Teacher* 38 (4): 418–23.

Evans, R. 1967. The usefulness of phonic generalizations above the primary grades. *The Reading Teacher* 20 (6): 419–25.

Flesch, R. 1955. *Why Johnny can't read*. New York: Harper and Row.

Fry, E. 1980. The new instant word list. *The Reading Teacher* 34 (3): 284–89.

Fry, E., and J. E. Kress. 2006. *The reading teacher's book of lists*. 5th ed. San Francisco: Jossey-Bass.

Garcia, G. 2008. Oral language development: Pedagogy and practice for English learners. *The California Reader* 41 (4): 10–23.

Gaskins, R. W., J. C. Gaskins, and I. W. Gaskins. 1991. A decoding program for poor readers—and the rest of the class, too! *Language Arts* 68 (3): 213–25.

Goodman, K. S. 1972. Reading: A psycholinguistic guessing game. In *Individualized reading instruction: A reader*, ed. L. A. Harris and C. B. Smith. New York: Holt, Rinehart, & Winston.

Graves, F., and S. M. Watts-Taffe. 2002. The place of word consciousness in a research based program. In *What research has to say about reading instruction*, ed. A. E. Farstrup and S. J. Samuels, 140–65. Newark, DE: International Reading Association.

Groff, P. 1986. The maturing of phonics instruction. *The Reading Teacher* 39 (9): 919–23.

Gunning, J. G. 1995. Word building: A strategic approach to the teaching of phonics. *The Reading Teacher* 48 (6): 484–88.

Hasbrouck, J. E., and G. Tindal. 1992. Curriculum-based oral reading fluency norms for students in grades 2 through 5. *Teaching Exceptional Children* 24 (3): 41–44.

Helman, L. A., and M. K. Burns. 2008. What does oral language have to do with it? Helping young English-language learners acquire a sight word vocabulary. *The Reading Teacher* 62 (1): 14–19.

Huey, E. B. 1908. *The psychology and pedagogy of reading*. New York: Macmillan.

International Reading Association. 1998. *Phonemic awareness and the teaching of reading: A position statement from the Board of Directors of the International Reading Association*. Newark, DE: International Reading Association.

Kuhn, M. 2004. Helping students become accurate, expressive readers: Fluency instruction for small groups. *The Reading Teacher* 58 (4): 338–44.

Manzo, A. V., and V. C. Manzo. 1995. *Teaching children to be literate: A reflective approach.* Fort Worth, TX: Harcourt Brace College Publishers.

National Endowment of the Arts. 2009. *Reading on the rise.* Washington, DC.

National Reading Panel. 2000. *Teaching children to read: An evidence-based assessment of the scientific research literature on reading and its implications for reading instruction* (National Institute of Health Publication No. 00-4769). Washington, DC: National Institute of Child Health and Human Development.

Opitz, M. F. 1995. *Getting the most from predictable books.* New York: Scholastic.

Padak, N., and T. Rasinski. 2008. *Fast start: Getting ready to read.* New York: Scholastic.

Peterson, C. L., D. C. Caverly, S. A. Nicholson, S. O'Neal and S. Cusenbary. 2000. *Building reading proficiency at the secondary school level: A guide to resources.* Retrieved September 25, 2003 from http://www.sedl.org.

Rhodes, L. K. 1981. I can read! Predictable books as a resource for reading and writing instruction. *The Reading Teacher* 34 (5): 511–18.

Roe, B. D., S. H. Smith, and P. C. Burns. 2005. *Teaching reading in today's elementary schools.* Boston: Houghton Mifflin.

Saccardi, M. C. 1996. Predictable books: Gateways to a lifetime of reading. *The Reading Teacher* 49 (7): 588–90.

Samuels, S. J. 1979. The method of repeated readings. *The Reading Teacher* 32 (4): 403–8.

———. 2003. Reading fluency: Its development and assessment. In *What research has to say about reading instruction*, ed. A. E. Farstrup and S. J. Samuels, 166–83 Newark, NJ: International Reading Association.

Schwanenflugel, P. J., E. B. Mersinger, J. Wisenbaker, M. Kuhn, and R. Morris. 2006. Becoming a fluent and automatic reader: A cross-sectional study. *Reading Research Quarterly* 41: 469–522.

Shannahan, T. 2008. Reading education through the eyes of a curmudgeon. *The California Reader* 42 (1).

Smith, N. B. 1967. *American Reading Instruction*. Newark, NJ: International Reading Association.

Stahl, S. A. 1992. Saying the 'p' word: Nine guidelines for exemplary phonics instruction. *The Reading Teacher* 45 (8): 618–25.

Stanovich, K. E. 1986. Matthew effects in reading: Some consequences of individual differences in the acquisition of literacy. *Reading Research Quarterly* 21 (3): 360–406.

Taylor, B. M., P. D. Pearson, D. S. Peterson, and M. C. Rodriguez. 2003. Reading growth in high-poverty classrooms: The influence of teacher practice encourage cognitive engagement in literacy learning. *The Elementary School Journal* 104 (1): 3–28.

Treiman, R., and V. Broderick. 1998. What's in a name: Children's knowledge about letters in their own names. *Journal of Experimental Child Psychology* 70 (2): 97–116.

Vogt, M., and J. Echevarria. 2008. *99 ideas and activities for teaching English learners with the SIOP model*. Boston: Pearson, Allyn, and Bacon.

White, T. G., J. Sowell, and A. Yanagihara. 1989. Teaching elementary students to use word-part clues. *The Reading Teacher* 42 (4): 302–8.

Wilfong, L. G. 2008. Building fluency, word recognition ability and confidence in struggling readers: The poetry academy. *The Reading Teacher* 62 (1): 4–13.

Wylie, R. E., and D. D. Durrell. 1970. Teaching vowels through phonograms. *Elementary English* 47 (6): 787–91.

Yopp, H. K. 1988. The validity and reliability of phonemic awareness tests. *Reading Research Quarterly* 23 (2): 159–77.

———. 1992. Developing phonemic awareness in young children. *The Reading Teacher* 45 (9): 696–704.

———.1995a. Read-aloud books for developing phonemic awareness: An annotated bibliography. *The Reading Teacher* 49 (6): 538–43.

———. 1995b. A test for assessing phonemic awareness in young children. *The Reading Teacher* 49 (1): 20–29.

Yopp, H. K. and L. Stapleton. 2008. Conciencia fonemica en Espanol (Phonemic awareness in Spanish). *The Reading Teacher* 61 (5): 374–82.

Yopp, H. K., R. H. Yopp, and A. Bishop. 2009. *Vocabulary instruction for academic success*. Huntington Beach, CA: Shell Education.

Children's Literature Cited

Alexander, M. 1981. *Move over, twerp*. New York: Dial.

———. 1999. *Blackboard bear*. New York: Candlewick.

Aliki. 1986. *Jack and Jake*. New York: William Morrow & Co.

Allard, H. 1977. *Miss Nelson is missing*. Boston: Houghton Mifflin.

———. 1977. *The Stupids step out*. Mooloolaba, Australia: Sandpiper.

Allard, H., and J. Marshall. 1985. *The Stupids die*. Mooloolaba, Australia: Sandpiper.

Andrews, J. 2003. *Very last first time*. Toronto: Groundwood Books.

Anno, M. 1988. *Anno's alphabet*. New York: Trophy Press.

Arnold, T. 1996. *No jumping on the bed*. New York: Puffin.

Asch, F. 1984. *Just like daddy*. New York: Aladdin.

————. 1990. *Sand cake.* New York: Grosset & Dunlap.

Baker, A. 1992. *Two tiny mice.* Boston: Kingfisher Books.

Bancheck, L. 1978. *Snake in, snake out.* New York: T. Y. Crowell.

Bang, M. 1985. *The paper crane.* New York: HarperCollins.

Barrett, J. 1985. *Cloudy with a chance of meatballs.* New York: Live Oak Media.

Barton, B. 1989. *Where's Al?* Mooloolaba, Australia: Sandpiper.

————. 1990. *Building a house.* New York: HarperTrophy.

Base, G. 1996. *Animalia.* New York: Puffin.

Bayer, H. 1992. *My name is Alice.* New York: Puffin.

Benchley, N. 1980. *Oscar otter.* New York: HarperCollins.

Berenstain, S., and J. Berenstain. 1994. *The bike lesson.* New York: Random House.

Bornstein, R. 1986. *Little gorilla.* Mooloolaba, Australia: Sandpiper.

Bragg, R. G. 1991. *Alphabet out loud.* New York: Simon & Schuster.

Branley, F. 1993. *It's raining cats and dogs: All kinds of weather and why we have it.* New York: Camelot.

————. 1999. *Flash, crash, rumble, and roll.* New York: HarperCollins.

Brandenburg, F. 1990. *I wish I was sick too.* New York: Mulberry Books.

Breinburg, P. 1974. *Shawn goes to school.* New York: T. Y. Crowell.

Brett, J. 1996. *Goldilocks and the three bears*. New York: Putnam.

Brown, M. W. 1989. *Wait till the moon is full*. New York: HarperTrophy.

———. 1993. *The quiet noisy book*. New York: HarperCollins.

———. 2005. *Goodnight moon*. New York: HarperCollins.

———. 2005. *The runaway bunny*. New York: HarperCollins.

Browne, A. 2008. *Willy the wimp*. New York: Walker Books, Ltd.

Buckley, H. 2000. *Grandfather and I*. New York: HarperCollins.

Buller, J., and S. Schade. 1990. *I love you, good night*. New York: Little Simon.

Burningham, J. 1995. *The dog*. New York: Candlewick.

———. 1995. *Mr. Gumpy's outing*. New York: Holt.

———. 1996. *The blanket*. New York: Candlewick.

———. 1996. *The friend*. New York: Candlewick.

———. 2000. *Avocado baby*. New York: Red Fox.

Burton, V. L. 1999. *Katy and the big snow*. Mooloolaba, Australia: Sandpiper.

Carle, E. 1989. *The very busy spider*. New York: Philomel

———. 1990. *The very quiet cricket*. New York: Philomel.

———. 1997. *The grouchy ladybug*. New York: Scholastic.

———. 1998. *Pancakes, pancakes*. New York: Aladdin.

———. 2005. *The very hungry caterpillar*. New York: Philomel.

Carlson, N. 1990. *I like me*. New York: Puffin.

Carroll, R. 1964. *Where's the bunny?* New York: HarperCollins.

Christelow, E. 1989. *Five little monkeys jumping on the bed.* New York: Scholastic.

Clifton, L. 1988. *Everett Anderson's goodbye.* New York: Holt.

Cohen, I. 1997. *ABC discovery!* New York: Dial Books for Young Readers.

Cohen, M. 2007. *Best friends.* New York: Aladdin.

———. 2009. *Will I have a friend?.* Long Island City, NY: Star Bright Books.

Cole, S. 1985. *When the tide is low.* New York: Harper Collins.

Cook, B. 2005. *The little fish that got away.* New York: HarperCollins.

Correlle, B. and K. Correlle. 1985. *Sarah's unicorn.* New York: HarperTrophy.

Crews, D. 1995. *Ten black dots.* New York: HarperTrophy.

dePaola, T. 1984. *The cloud book.* New York: Holiday House.

———. 1985. *Tomie dePaola's Mother Goose.* New York: Putnam.

———. 1998. *The knight and the dragon.* New York: Putnam.

de Regniers, B., B. Schenk, M. White, and J. Bennett. 1988. *Sing a song of popcorn.* London: Hodder Children's Books.

Delton, J. 1979. *The new girl at school.* New York: Dutton Children's Books.

Deming, A. G. 1994. *Who is tapping at my window?* New York: Puffin.

Dewdney, A. 2007. *Llama, Llama mad at mama*. New York: HarperCollins.

Dunbar, J. 1999. *Seven sillies*. New York: Red Fox Books.

Dunrea, O. 1990. *Mogwogs on the march*. New York: Holiday.

Eastman, P. D. 1960. *Are you my mother?* New York: Random House.

Ehlert, L. 1994. *Eating the alphabet: Fruits and vegetables from A to Z*. San Diego, CA: Harcourt.

Emberley, R. 1998. *Three cool kids*. Boston: Little Brown.

Ernst, L. C. 1986. *Up to ten and down again*. New York: HarperCollins.

Ets, M. H. 1978. *Gilberto and the wind*. New York: Puffin

Feczko, K. 1987. *Umbrella parade*. Mahwah, NJ: Troll.

Flack, M. 1971. *Ask Mr. Bear*. New York: Aladdin.

———. 1997. *Angus and the cat*. New York: Farrar, Straus, and Giroux.

Fleming, D. 2002. *Alphabet under construction*. New York: Holt.

Fox, M. 2005. *Hattie and the fox*. New York: Aladdin.

Freeman, D. 1989. *A pocket for Corduroy*. New York: Puffin.

Gag, W. 2006. *Millions of cats*. New York: Puffin.

Galdone, P. 1973. *The little red hen*. New York: Scholastic.

———. 1986. *The teeny tiny woman*. Mooloolaba, Australia: Sandpiper.

Geraghty, P. 1993. *Stop that noise!* New York: Knopf.

Gerson, M. J. 1995. *Why the sky is far away.* Boston: Little Brown.

Gerstein, M. 1988. *Roll over!* New York: Knopf.

Gibbons, G. 1988. *Dinosaurs, dragonflies, and diamonds.* New York: Atheneum.

Ginsberg, M. 1988. *The chick and the duckling.* New York: Aladdin.

Godkin, C. 2001. *What about ladybugs?* San Francisco, CA: Sierra Club.

Gordon, J. 1991. *Six sleepy sheep.* New York: Trumpet.

Grey, J. 1989. *Yummy, yummy.* Mahway, NY: Troll.

Griffith, H. 1980. *Mine will, said John.* New York: Greenwillow.

———. 1982. *Alex and the cat.* New York: Greenwillow.

Hall, D. 2004. *Ox-cart man.* New York: Live Oak Media.

Henkes, K. 1996. *Lilly's purple plastic purse.* New York: HarperCollins.

———. 1996. *Sheila Rae, the brave.* New York: HarperTrophy.

Hill, E. 2003. *Where's Spot?* New York: Puffin.

Hoban, R. and L. Hoban. 1992. *The Stone Doll of Sister Brute.* New York: Dell Yearling.

Hoban, T. 1995. *26 letters and 99 cents.* New York: Mulberry Books.

Hoberman, M. A. 2007. *A house is a house for me.* New York: Puffin.

Hopkins, L. B. 1987. *The sky is full of song.* New York: Trophy Press.

Hutchins, P. 1986. *1 hunter*. New York: HarperCollins.

———. 1991. *The surprise party*. New York: Aladdin.

———. 1993. *The wind blew*. New York: Aladdin.

———. 2000. *Little pink pig*. New York: HarperTrophy.

Jenkins, S. 1997. *Biggest, strongest, fastest*. Mooloolaba, Australia: Sandpiper.

Johnston, T. 1989. *The adventures of mole and troll*. New York: Dell Yearling.

———. 1989. *Night noises and other mole and troll stories*. New York: Dell Yearling.

Kantrowitz, M. 1989. *Willy bear*. New York: Aladdin.

Keats, E. J. 1998. *Goggles!* New York: Puffin.

———. 2005. *Whistle for Willie*. New York: Live Oak Media.

Kellogg, S. 2002. *Pinkerton behave*. New York: Dial.

Kitchen, B. 1991. *Animal alphabet*. Cambridge, England: Lutterworth Press.

Kraus, R. 1987. *Herman the helper*. New York: Aladdin.

———. 1994. *Leo the late bloomer*. New York: HarperCollins.

———. 2000. *Whose mouse are you?* New York: Simon & Schuster.

Krauss, R. 2003. *I can fly*. New York: Golden Books.

Langstaff, J. 1991. *Oh, a hunting we will go*. New York: Aladdin.

Larrick, N. 1993. *When the dark comes dancing*. New York: Trophy Press.

Lester, H. 2006. *Tacky the penguin*. Boston: Houghton Mifflin.

Lewison, W. 1992. *Buzz said the bee*. New York: Cartwheel.

Lionni, L. 1967. *Frederick*. New York: Pantheon Books.

———. 1973. *Swimmy*. New York: Dragonfly Books.

———. 1995. *Little blue and little yellow*. New York: HarperTrophy.

Lobel, A. 1988. *Small pig*. New York: HarperTrophy.

MacDonald, E. 1993. *Mike's kite*. New York: Harcourt.

MacDonald, R. 2003. *Achoo! Bang! The noisy alphabet*. Brookfield, CT: Roaring Brook.

Mack, S. 1974. *Ten bears in my bed*. New York: Knopf.

Marshall, J. 1986. *The cut-ups*. New York: Puffin.

———. 2008. *George and Martha*. New York: Houghton Mifflin.

Martin, B. Jr. 1971. *Fire, fire, said Mrs. McGuire*. San Diego: Harcourt Brace.

———. 2007. *Brown bear, brown bear, what do you see?* New York: Holt.

Martin, B. Jr., and J. Archambault. 2000. *Chicka chicka boom boom*. New York: Aladdin.

Mayer, M. 1992. *There's a nightmare in my closet*. New York: Puffin.

———. 1992. *There's something in my attic*. New York: Puffin.

McCloskey, R. 2004. *Make way for ducklings*. New York: Live Oak Media.

McDermott, G. 1996. *Zomo the rabbit*. San Diego, CA: Voyager Books.

McKissack, P. C. 1986. *Flossie and the Fox*. New York: Dial.

Morris, A. 1995. *Houses and homes*. New York: HarperTrophy.

Most, B. 1992. *There's an ant in Anthony*. New York: HarperCollins.

Noble, T. 1992. *The day Jimmy's boa ate the wash*. New York: Puffin.

Nodset, J. 1963. *Who took the farmer's hat?* New York: HarperCollins.

Numeroff, L. J. 1985. *If you give a moose a muffin*. New York: HarperCollins.

———. 2000. *If you give a pig a pancake*. New York: HarperCollins.

———. 2000. *If you take a mouse to the movies*. New York: HarperCollins.

———. 2005. *If you give a pig a party*. New York: HarperCollins.

———. 2007. *If you give a mouse a cookie*. New York: Harper Festival.

Oppenheim, J. 1999. *Have you seen trees?* New York: Scholastic.

Otto, C. 2007. *Dinosaur chase*. New York: Red Fox.

Oxenbury, H. 1981. *Friends*. New York: Little Simon.

———. 2004. *The Helen Oxenbury nursery story book*. New York: Knopf.

Palmer, H. 1984. *A fish out of water*. New York: HarperCollins.

Payne, E. 1973. *Katy no-pocket*. Mooloolaba, Australia: Sandpiper.

Peet. B. 1984. *Big bad Bruce*. New York: Houghton Mifflin.

————. 1989. *Zella, Zack, and Zodiac*. Mooloolaba, Australia: Sandpiper.

Pfister, M. 2000. *The rainbow fish*. New York: Scholastic.

Pizer, A. 1992. *It's a perfect day*. Glenview, IL: Scott Foresman.

Prelutsky, J. 1983. *The Random House book of poetry for children*. New York: Random House.

————. 1986. *Read aloud rhymes for the very young*. New York: Knopf.

————. 1990. *Something big has been here*. New York: Greenwillow.

Rey, H. A. 1995. *Curious George*. Boston: Houghton Mifflin.

Rounds, G. 1990. *I know an old lady who swallowed a fly*. New York: Holiday House.

Schmidt, K. 1985. *The gingerbread man*. New York: Scholastic.

Segal, L. 1989. *Tell me a trudy*. New York: Farrar, Straus, & Giroux.

Sendak, M. 1988. *Where the wild things are*. New York: HarperCollins.

————. 1991. *Chicken soup with rice*. New York: HarperCollins.

Serfozo, M. 1993. *Rain talk*. New York: Aladdin.

Seuss, Dr. 1963. *Hop on pop*. New York: Random House.

————. 1965. *Fox in socks*. New York: Random House.

————. 1987. *The cat in the hat*. New York: Random House.

————. 1988. *Green eggs and ham*. New York: Random House.

————. 2006. *The cat in the hat comes back*. New York: Random House.

Shaw, N. 1992. *Sheep in a shop*. Mooloolaba, Australia: Sandpiper.

————. 1996. *Sheep in a ship*. Boston: Houghton Mifflin.

Silverstein, S. 1964. *A giraffe and a half*. New York: HarperCollins.

————. 2004. *Where the sidewalk ends*. New York HarperCollins.

————. 2005. *Runny babbit*. New York: HarperCollins.

Slepian, J., and A. Seidler. 2001. *The hungry thing*. New York: Scholastic.

Slobodkina, E. 1997. *Caps for sale*. New York: HarperTrophy.

Steig, W. 2005. *Sylvester and the magic pebble*. New York: Simon & Schuster.

Taback, S. 1997. *There was an old lady who swallowed a fly*. New York: Viking Juvenile.

Tashjian, V. 1995. *Juba this and Juba that*. Boston: Little Brown.

Tryon, L. 1991. *Albert's alphabet*. New York: Atheneum.

Udry, J. M. 1988. *Let's be enemies*. New York: HarperCollins.

————. 2001. *Thump and plunk*. New York: HarperTrophy.

Van Allsburg, C. 1987. *The Z was zapped*. Boston: Houghton Mifflin.

Viorst, J. 1987. *Alexander and the terrible, horrible, no good, very bad day*. New York: Macmillan.

———. 1997. *The alphabet from Z to A (with much confusion on the way)*. New York: Aladdin.

Waber, B. 1993. *Lyle, Lyle, crocodile.* Boston: Houghton Mifflin

———. 2008. *Ira sleeps over.* Mooloolaba, Australia: Sandpiper.

Waddell, M. 2007. *The pig in the pond.* New York: Walker Books.

Walsh, E. S. 1996. *Hop, jump.* San Diego, CA: Voyager Books.

Walton, R. 1995. *Once there was a bull...(frog).* Layton, UT: Gibbs Smith.

Weiss, L. 1985. *My teacher sleeps in school.* New York: Puffin.

Wellington, M. 1992. *The sheep follow.* New York: Dutton.

Wells, R. 2000. *Noisy Nora.* New York: Puffin.

West, C. 2009. *Have you seen the crocodile?* London: Walker Books Ltd.

Williams, V. 1984. *A chair for my mother.* New York: HarperTrophy.

Wood, A. 1993. *Little penguin's tale.* Boston: Voyager Books.

———. 2004. *The napping house.* San Diego: Harcourt Brace.

———. 2007. *Silly Sally.* Boston: Red Wagon Books.

Wormell, C. 2004. *New alphabet of animals.* Philadelphia, PA: Running Press Kids.

Yashima, M. 1977. *Momo's kitten.* New York: Live Oak Media.

Yashima, T. 1986. *Umbrella.* New York: Puffin.

Yolen, J. 1997. *All in the woodland early: An ABC book.* Honesdale, PA: Boyds Mills Press.